NULLING
OUT

THE TERRIFYING COST OF SUCCESS AND THE PATH BACK TO BEING FULLY ALIVE

—

BY CHERYL JACK, MD

NULLING OUT

THE TERRIFYING COST OF SUCCESS AND THE PATH BACK TO BEING FULLY ALIVE

DISCLAIMER NOTICE.

This book is sold with the understanding that the author is not engaged in rendering medical, psychological, or other professional services. The insights and strategies shared are for informational purposes only. If you require personal assistance or advice, please consult a competent professional.

The individuals, case studies, and stories depicted in this work are composites, drawn from real-world patterns observed over the author's four decades of experience. To protect the privacy of all involved, these stories have been fictionalized. All names, identifying details, and circumstances have been altered to accurately represent the phenomenon of "nulling out." Any resemblance to actual persons, living or deceased, is coincidental.

Certain images are licensed from Adobe Stock and Shutterstock.

To the thousands of individuals who, over forty years, bravely navigated an unnamed darkness and, in doing so, taught me everything that is in these pages.

This book is my promise to them fulfilled.

TABLE OF CONTENTS

INTRODUCTION: INTO THE DARKNESS

There is a crisis happening in plain sight, and no one is talking about it.

If you walk into any country club, boardroom, or affluent neighborhood, you see them: extremely successful people who've seemingly accomplished everything they were meant to—or at least intended to. They drive the best cars, live in the nicest houses, and hold the most impressive titles. Their LinkedIn profiles glow and read like an Inc. success story. Their bank accounts reflect decades of wise decisions and hard work.

And they are slowly disappearing.

Not physically—they show up, perform, and deliver results. But the person inside the achievement is vanishing, one accomplished day at a time. They are becoming ghosts in their own lives, high-performing shells of who they once were.

I call this phenomenon "nulling out," and in my forty-plus years of working with people, I've watched it claim some of our brightest minds and strongest leaders. Unlike burnout, which announces itself through exhaustion and declining performance, nulling out is invisible. These individuals continue to excel while going dark internally.

This book is about that darkness, and more importantly, about finding a way back to the light.

Jason built a multimillion dollar company and is at the top of his game, but he struggles to recall the last time he felt truly excited about anything. Mark climbed to the C-suite, but can't leave work at the door; he speaks to his own family like he's conducting a business meeting. Patrick got what he was after, achieving his dream of financial freedom only to feel like a prisoner in a cage, trapped in a life that looked perfect only from the outside.

These aren't isolated cases. They represent a silent epidemic that's gutting our most accomplished individuals from the inside out.

For decades, we've focused on burnout, depression, and anxiety – conditions that usually announce themselves through clear symptoms and declining performance. But nulling out happens in the shadows. It allows its victims to maintain their productivity while slowly erasing everything that makes them human.

The consequences are devastating, not just for the individuals involved, but for their families, their organizations, and society as a whole. When our highest performers become emotional voids, they not only lose themselves but also lose the capacity to truly lead, genuinely connect, and model what success actually looks like.

This book will take you through the anatomy of this crisis: how nulling out happens, why it's more dangerous emotionally than any condition we currently recognize, what the warning signs look like, and, most importantly, how to find a way back to yourself without losing everything you've built.

You've picked up this book, so chances are you recognize something of yourself in these pages. Maybe you've achieved everything you strove for, only to find a gaping void as your reward. Maybe you're surrounded by the trappings of success but feel incredibly alone. Maybe you're crushing it on paper, performing at high levels while feeling empty inside.

You are not broken. You are not ungrateful. You are not having a midlife crisis.

You are nulled out. And that is fixable.

Let's begin.

PART I
THE CRISIS

"You can be the most successful person in the room
and a complete stranger to yourself."

CHAPTER 1
THE SILENT EPIDEMIC NO ONE IS TALKING ABOUT

*"What is not brought to consciousness,
comes to us as fate."*
Carl Jung

David sat in his corner office, taking in the gorgeous view over the Pacific, as he reflected on what he had achieved. He had everything he'd dreamed of having by age forty-five: senior partnership at a prestigious consulting firm, an upper six-figure salary, respect from his colleagues, and a beautiful home in the suburbs. His calendar was packed with important meetings, and his opinions shaped million-dollar decisions. That morning, his team celebrated landing their biggest client yet. David smiled, shook hands, said all the right things.

But he felt nothing.

Meanwhile, in another part of the country, Grant received the promotion he'd been working towards for five years—the one that would set him up for early retirement. His team threw a celebration lunch. His family sent congratulatory texts. His LinkedIn notifications blew up with praise. But later, parked alone in his car in the empty garage, Grant sat in silence. He stared ahead vacantly... and felt absolutely nothing.

Evan, a successful software engineer and single parent of two, stared blankly at the lukewarm coffee in his mug. His children bounced around in the next room, having everything they needed, and were thriving. Evan had just won an award for building an advanced AI system which put his company at the forefront. He told everyone, "This is just the beginning." Yet in that kitchen, his words felt hollow. Evan felt distant, as if he were watching life go on through a pane of glass, emotionally disconnected.

David, Grant, and Evan have different lives, but they all suffer from the same thing: the silent epidemic no one is talking about but should be. They are the face, the epitome of what this affliction looks like. It is insidious, creeping in and taking no prisoners. It's like waking up one morning to find the ground beneath you has slightly shifted, so over time, you start sinking without even realizing it. Before they knew it, it had taken their zest, their hearts, their souls. As quick as stepping into a sinkhole, but far less dramatic. This epidemic is a crisis of the self. I call it "nulling out." Many men and women are lost to it.

What happened? These high-functioning professionals have optimized themselves into emotional voids. They meet every external measure of success while experiencing an internal famine that threatens to consume everything meaningful in their lives.

Nulling out occurs gradually, almost imperceptibly, one small compromise at a time. One genuine desire is sacrificed for practical considerations; one personal preference is set aside for professional advancement, and so on until there's nothing left but the ghost of life. Nulling out erases the person you were and leaves behind only the high-functioning machine.

David, Grant, and Evan aren't isolated cases. They represent a growing crisis. In my four decades of working with high achievers, I've watched this phenomenon accelerate. What used to be an occasional case of successful individuals feeling disconnected has become a pervasive pattern. The very systems that create external success are systematically destroying internal life.

This phenomenon is reflected in the growing demand for executive coaching, as leaders struggle to reconnect with their true selves. Employee engagement scores continue to plummet even as productivity soars. The most successful demographic in human history reports the highest levels of existential emptiness. We are creating human performance machines at the expense of human beings.

The technology executive who built three startups but can't remember what initially excited him about innovation. The surgeon who saves lives daily but feels dead inside. The attorney who wins every case but has lost all sense of justice. The financial advisor who grows everyone else's wealth while feeling emotionally bankrupt.

They all ask the same haunting question: "Is this all there is?"

The most chilling part? The disconnect. Most nulled-out individuals don't even realize what's happening to them. They assume the emptiness is the price of success, that it is inevitable.

They're wrong.

Consider what happens when our decision-makers operate from emotional voids:

The pharmaceutical executive who approves price increases that hurt patients because he's disconnected from the human impact of his choices. The tech leader who builds addictive platforms because he's lost touch with what a healthy human connection actually feels like. The financial executive who creates predatory products because he's so far removed from his own values that he can't recognize exploitation. These aren't evil people making malicious choices. They are nulled-out individuals operating from a place of such profound internal emptiness that they have lost the capacity to consider the human cost of their decisions.

When success becomes separated from soul, we do not just get empty individuals—we get empty institutions, empty policies, and empty solutions to problems that require deeply human responses.

The climate crisis, political polarization, economic inequality, and social isolation—these challenges require leaders who can think beyond metrics, who can connect with something larger than just optimization, who retain some spark of the idealism and creativity that originally drove them toward achievement.

We can't solve human problems with human machines.

And yet that's exactly what we're creating, one optimized professional at a time, and the window for intervention is rapidly closing.

Every day that nulling out goes unrecognized, more of our brightest minds slip further into the void. Every promotion that rewards performance over humanity pushes another leader deeper into disconnection. Every success story that celebrates achievement while ignoring the individual behind it reinforces the very patterns that create this epidemic.

The real tragedy isn't just that these individuals are suffering—it's that they don't know they're suffering. They've been so thoroughly conditioned to equate emptiness with success that they mistake their numbness for professional maturity, their disconnection for necessary focus.

They believe this is simply what winning looks like.

But here's what makes addressing this crisis particularly urgent: nulled-out individuals don't stay stable. The human psyche cannot operate in a complete void indefinitely. When someone feels nothing

for long enough, they will eventually do anything to feel something, even if it destroys everything they've built.

The stable executive who suddenly has an affair that destroys his marriage; the disciplined entrepreneur who makes reckless investments that tank his company; the careful professional who

starts drinking or gambling compulsively. These are not random midlife meltdowns but predictable consequences of prolonged internal emptiness.

When you null out for too long, the pressure to feel something, anything, real or otherwise becomes overwhelming, and the choices you make because of that desperation are rarely wise.

The cost is mounting: destroyed families, ruined careers, squandered potential, and organizations led by people who have not only forgotten what their mission and values were, but what it means to be human.

Perhaps the most troubling part is what we're modeling for the next generation. Young professionals who watch their successful elders may conclude that emptiness is the inevitable price for achievement. They start optimizing themselves for metrics rather than meaning, performance rather than fulfillment.

We're not just creating a generation of nulled-out leaders; we're creating a culture that views nulling out as normal, even desirable.

This has to change.

The good news is that nulling out is entirely reversible. It's not a chemical imbalance requiring medication. It's not a personality disorder requiring years of therapy. It's not a character flaw needing moral reformation.

It's a disconnection that can be reconnected. A void that can be filled. An erasure that can be undone.

However, in order to achieve this, we first have to name it (we just did), recognize it, understand exactly what we're dealing with and why our current approaches fail to address it.

The man who feels nothing while achieving everything isn't broken—he's just nulled out. The husband who provides for everyone while slowly disappearing isn't ungrateful—he's lost the connection to himself. The man who's at the top of his career but can't enjoy his family isn't experiencing depression or a midlife crisis—he can no longer feel human emotion. The leader who can execute strategy but can't remember why any of it matters isn't lacking vision—he's been systematically optimized out of his own life.

These individuals don't have to lower their standards or abandon their ambitions. They don't have to choose between success and satisfaction, achievement and authenticity.

They simply need to understand what happened to them, why it happened, and how to rebuild the connection between who they are and what they do.

They need to understand that emptiness isn't a natural consequence of success.

In the next chapter, you'll see how nulling out is different and how knowing that is the key to gaining control over your life.

You can have both: the success you've built and the person you used to be. You can achieve at the highest levels while feeling genuinely alive.

You just need to remember how.

CHAPTER 2
WHAT IS NULLING OUT?

"The most powerful weapon against stress is our ability to choose one thought over another."
William James

Dr. Thompson made his first incision at 7:23 a.m. He worked methodically through the procedure and completed yet another successful surgery. When he stepped back from the operating table, he glanced at the heart monitor and then at the clock: done in two hours and forty-seven minutes. He walked to the scrub sink to wash his hands, and all he could think of was the word, "next."

Somewhere along the line, he lost his passion for healing, his connection to his patients' stories, and his investment in his life-saving work. Dr. Thompson had become a technician, and a highly paid one to boot.

Dr. Thompson is experiencing what many high performers are. It isn't depression, it isn't burnout, it isn't a new mental illness. It is a condition we currently do not recognize or treat; a disconnect. They're experiencing something that requires its own definition, its own understanding, and its own approach to healing.

To solve a problem, you first have to name it accurately. For too long, we've been using the wrong names for what's happening to our highest achievers.

Nulling out is the gradual erasure of your authentic self in service of external performance, resulting in high-functioning individuals who maintain high productivity while experiencing complete internal emptiness. This isn't a new condition, but it is reaching epidemic levels, supercharged by a relentless hustle culture that mistakes constant activity for real achievement. This often leads to the quiet disintegration of a person's inner world.

WHAT DOES "AUTHENTIC SELF" MEAN?

The word has been worn down by overuse, often mistaken for radical honesty without regard for impact, or a license to be impulsive. This is not what I mean when I refer to the authentic self.

In this context, authenticity is not a personality trait you either have or don't. It is the capacity to access and act upon your own genuine, internal signals. It's that simple, and that profound.

Your authentic self is the part of you that has:

- **Genuine Preferences:** It knows, on a gut level, what it wants and what it doesn't want, separate from what is logical or expected.

- **Spontaneous Responses:** It generates real, unscripted emotional and intellectual reactions to the world—joy, anger, curiosity, boredom, outrage, excitement.

- **An Internal Compass:** It has a set of core values that create an internal sense of "rightness" and "wrongness" that exists independent of exter-nal rules or rewards.

Authenticity is not about being unfiltered; it is about having a filter of your own making. Nulling out is the process of systematically decommissioning this internal guidance system and replacing it with an external one built on optimization and expectation. Reconnection, therefore, is the methodical work of bringing it back online.

Imagine a highly sophisticated computer that can run any program flawlessly, but someone has deleted the operating system that gives it personality, preferences, and purpose. The machine still works perfectly; it processes information, completes tasks, and delivers results. But there's no consciousness driving the choices, no authentic decision-making happening beneath the surface.

That is what happens to nulled-out individuals. They become human operating systems without the core programming that makes them uniquely themselves.

THE ANATOMY OF A NULLED-OUT LIFE

For a nulled-out person, the day begins with function, not feeling. The alarm goes off, and they rise with practiced efficiency. There is no joy in the day ahead, and there is no dread. They sleep well but wake up with the sensation of moving through life underwater.

Decisions are calculated, not felt. When asked what they want for breakfast, they genuinely have no answer. The part of them that holds preferences is offline. They choose the 'optimal' option—the healthy, efficient one—and eat without truly savoring the flavor.

At work, their performance is a model of excellence. They execute complex strategies, meet every deadline, and are admired by colleagues for their unshakable composure. Their thinking has become a hyper-focused algorithm, completely divorced from any sense of purpose. They can explain how to achieve the goal, but they have long forgotten why it should matter. This is their most defining and insidious trait: functional perfection wrapped around a profound internal void.

Social interactions are a masterclass in performance. Their relationships have been automated. They ask the right questions in meetings, laugh at the appropriate moments, and provide thoughtful, scripted responses to their families in the evening. They have become so skilled at performing normalcy that even the people closest to them rarely notice anything is wrong. They are the stable, reliable center, all while feeling as if they are operating their own body remotely, watching a stranger live their life.

By the end of the day, time itself feels artificial. The days blur into one another, and nothing feels distinct enough to form a memory. They are living in a perpetual present, disconnected from both the satisfaction of the past and the anticipation of the future. It is a life perfected into a state of profound, functional emptiness.

HOW NULLING OUT DEVELOPS: A SLOW FADE

Nulling out doesn't strike suddenly; it's the result of a thousand tiny choices made over years.

It begins innocently. A talented individual learns that certain responses get rewarded while others don't. They discover that being agreeable is more valuable than being authentic, that being efficient matters more than being engaged, and that being consistent is prized over being creative.

So, they begin to optimize. They suppress the parts of themselves that don't contribute to the performance and amplify the parts that do. At first, this feels like growth. It feels like becoming more professional, more effective.

But optimization has a cost. Each time they choose the "correct" response over the authentic one, each time they prioritize the expected over the desired, they are telling a part of themselves to go offline.

At first, these parts just go quiet. But if you ignore something long enough, it stops trying to get your attention. The creative impulses, the spontaneous desires, the real reactions—they don't vanish right away. They fade, like a radio signal moving slowly out of range.

The person doesn't even notice what's being lost, because the performance is still running perfectly. Their work improves. Their relationships appear stable. By every external metric, their life is a success. Why would they ever question a system that is clearly working?

This is why nulling out goes undetected. Colleagues see a reliable high-performer. Family members see someone who meets every obligation. Doctors see a person with good vital signs and no obvious distress. The individuals themselves, measuring their well-being by their bank account and their career progress, believe they should feel good.

But "should feel good" and "actually feeling good" are entirely different. And when you've spent years optimizing for external validation, you can lose the ability to even tell the difference.

Understanding what nulling out is requires understanding what it is not. Because it looks so much like success from the outside, it is easy to mistake for something else entirely. In the next chapter, we'll draw clear lines between nulling out and the conditions it's often confused with.

CHAPTER 3
HOW NULLING OUT DIFFERS FROM EVERYTHING ELSE

"We know what we are, but know not what we may be."
William Shakespeare

Michael sat in his car, feeling unsettled. His hands trembled on the steering wheel as waves of fear and anxiety washed over him. I feel like I'm dying. What's wrong with me? he thought. Convinced that something was wrong, he drove to the hospital at 2:00 a.m. The ER doctor examined him and found nothing abnormal. But Michael was not convinced. After more tests, the physician sent him home with a referral to a psychiatrist. He was subsequently diagnosed with depression and started on medication.

Six months later, Michael was still on the same medication but felt no improvement. He continued to function well at work, but his sense of emptiness had only grown stronger. Michael wasn't depressed. He was emotionally disconnected. Without the proper language for it, he was treated for the wrong condition, with predictably poor results.

THE ONGOING PROBLEM OF DIAGNOSTIC CONFUSION

Professional counselors and therapists have long relied on the Diagnostic and Statistical Manual (DSM) for clarification. Inside this tome are categories for countless conditions, but nothing that captures the experience of high-functioning internal emptiness. When someone performs well but feels completely empty inside, our current frameworks fall short. This gap is caused by how mental health is defined.

Most mental health problems show up as struggling to work, connect with others, or think clearly. Nulling out does the opposite: people may work even better, but their inner life fades away. This is a hidden cost of being "high functioning." Values and traits like discipline, efficiency, and the ability to perform under pressure are often required to succeed, but can also conceal the emptiness underneath.

Cultural, organizational, and family systems reinforce this pattern.

Cultural pressure to maintain a 'successful' persona can occur at the expense of personal well-being. Workplaces may focus on productivity as being paramount over well-being, failing to recognize or care about the signs of emotional disconnection. Family systems may unknowingly reinforce expectations to perform and succeed while ignoring emotional needs.

This contributes to the difficulty in recognizing and treating nulling out effectively. Reflecting on societal success indicators creates a foundation for exploring how to reconnect meaningfully later. For now, let's compare nulling out with other common conditions it is confused with, starting with burnout.

BURNOUT: WHEN THE ENGINE OVERHEATS VS. WHEN THE DRIVER DISAPPEARS

Burnout has become a catch-all explanation, but its true fingerprint is one of depletion, not emotion. It is a crisis of capacity, a profound state of chronic exhaustion directly linked to an overwhelming workload. The defining characteristic isn't a vague feeling of being 'off,' but a pointed cynicism and corrosive resentment aimed squarely at the demands of the job.

For the compulsive high achiever, this internal depletion rarely leads to an immediate drop in performance. Instead, they begin to burn the candle at both ends, sacrificing their well-being to maintain the same high standard of external results. They operate on sheer will, even as their internal fuel tank runs dry. Physically, the body bears the cost, manifesting this chronic stress through headaches, insomnia, and fatigue. In burnout, the equation is always clear: the workload is the problem, and the individual is sacrificing themselves to solve it.

Thematic Intensity Comparison

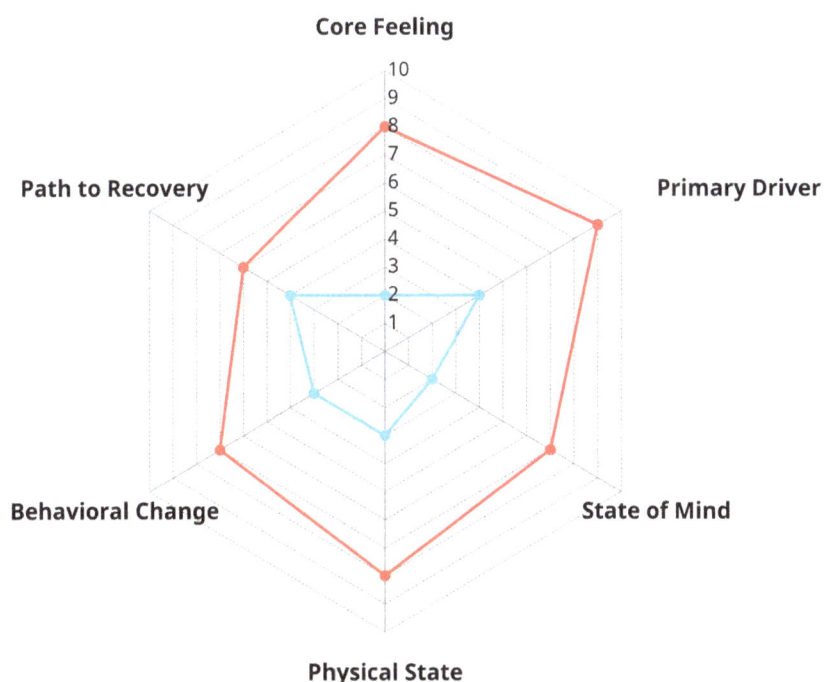

Score Comparison

As the charts show, burnout is a high-energy crisis of depletion—the engine is overheating, running on sheer will. Note the high intensity of the 'Primary Driver' and 'Physical State.' In contrast, the nulled-out state is a crisis of connection where the driver has simply disappeared—the engine is cool, and the will to steer is gone.

The difference here is crucial. A burned-out executive complains about unreasonable deadlines and dreams of vacation; they still have a functioning compass but are exhausted from paddling against a current. A nulled-out executive meets every deadline, works efficiently, feels indifferent when vacation time comes, and is adrift on a calm sea with a broken compass.

This is why conventional treatments for burnout not only fail to help a nulled-out person, but can sometimes make the feelings of emptiness even worse.

Burnout	Aspect	Nulling Out
Over-engagement and exhaustion. A feeling of being drained, frantic, and emotionally overwhelmed.	Core Feeling	Disengagement and apathy. A feeling of being empty, numb, and emotionally flat.
Excessive and prolonged stress, often work-related. Too many demands, not enough resources.	Primary Driver	A chronic defense mechanism against overwhelm. A gradual shutdown of emotional and cognitive systems.
Hyper-engaged and agitated. Constant worry, anxiety, and a sense of urgency and panic.	State of Mind	Disengaged and quiet. A lack of internal chatter, worry, or strong emotional response.
Characterized by fatigue, stress-related symptoms like headaches, and sleep disturbances.	Physical State	Often presents as low energy or lethargy, but without the acute symptoms of stress. A state of low arousal.
Leads to cynicism, detachment from work, and reduced professional efficacy. A feeling of 'I can't do this anymore.'	Behavioral Change	Leads to a quiet withdrawal from life, reduced ambition, and a lack of engagement in personal or professional goals. A feeling of 'I don't care.'
Requires disengagement, rest, setting boundaries, and managing stressors. Focus is on recharging.	Path to Recovery	Requires re-engagement, finding meaning, and reigniting passion. Focus is on reconnecting with self and world.

TREATING BURNOUT: RESTORING CAPACITY

The treatment for true burnout is a direct response to its cause: depletion. Think of it as a profound drain of what can only be described as life-force energy. The primary goal is to restore these depleted physical, cognitive, and emotional resources.

Effective strategies often involve a multi-pronged approach. This includes establishing firm boundaries to protect time and energy, delegating responsibilities to reduce overwhelming workloads, and, crucially, engaging in genuine rest. This can range from taking a true vacation without work interruptions to implementing daily practices that allow for mental and physical recovery.

However, sometimes these individual strategies are not enough. If the work environment itself is fundamentally untenable—if the demands are chronically unreasonable and the leadership is unwilling to change the system—then the most effective and courageous treatment for burnout is to change the environment itself. This can mean seeking a different role within the organization or, if necessary, finding new employment altogether. The core principle is simple: to refill a system that has been completely drained, you must first stop the leak, even if it means leaving the ship.

Now, let's examine how depression differs from nulling out.

DEPRESSION: WHEN THE WORLD GOES DARK VS. WHEN YOU UNPLUG AND TUNE OUT

Depression is not just sadness; it's 's the emotional equivalent of a gray filter being placed over the world.

The primary symptoms are often a persistent feeling of hopelessness or irritability, but the true hallmark of a major depressive episode is anhedonia: the profound inability to feel pleasure. The world loses its color. Food loses its taste, and laughter feels like a distant memory.

This internal grayness seeps outward, disrupting the body's natural rhythms with changes to sleep, appetite, and energy. Cognitively, it creates a fog that makes it difficult to concentrate or make decisions. This is often accompanied by deep feelings of worthlessness or guilt, and in its darkest forms, can lead to thoughts of death. It is a debilitating condition that directly impairs one's ability to engage with work, relationships, and life itself.

Thematic Intensity Comparison

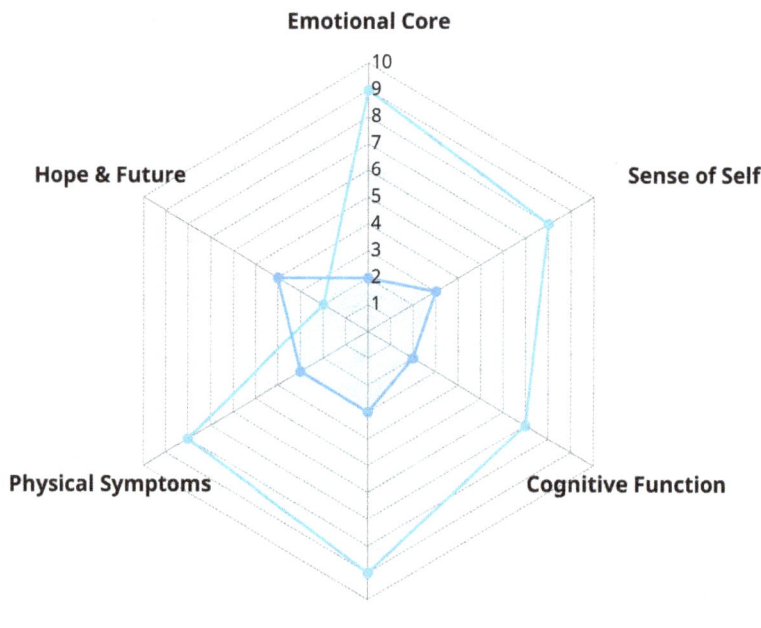

Source of Pain

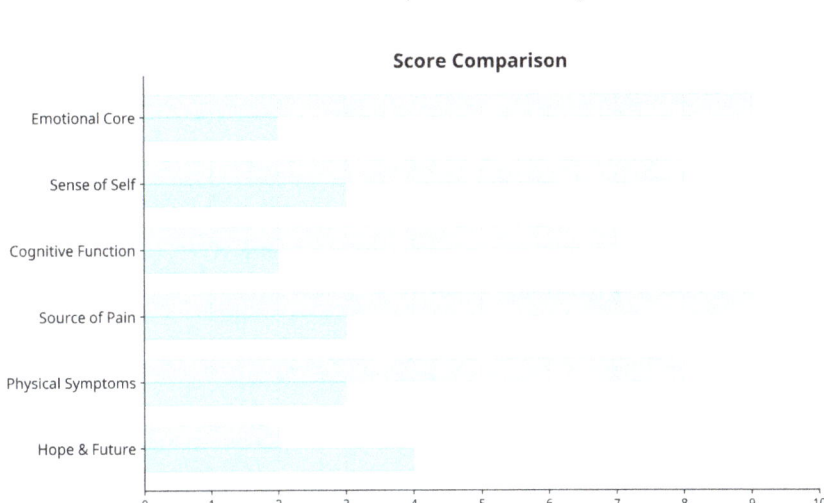

Depression   Nulling Out

Score Comparison

These charts highlight the critical difference between the presence of heavy negative emotion and its absence. Depression is a state of high-intensity suffering, defined by a powerful 'Source of Pain' and loss of 'Hope.' The nulled-out state is characterized by a void—an erasure of both the positive and the negative.

The experience of depression is one of profound and heavy suffering. It is a condition that drains the world of its color, making it a monumental struggle simply to get out of bed or engage with work and relationships. Because of its direct impact on mood, energy, and self-worth, a multi-faceted approach to treatment is often required to lift the oppressive gray filter and help a person reconnect with their life.

Depression	Aspect	Nulling Out
Profound sadness, emptiness, and anhedonia (inability to feel pleasure). A heavy weight of negative emotion.	Emotional Core	Emotional numbness and apathy. A profound lack of both positive and negative emotions. A void.
Often involves feelings of worthlessness, guilt, and self-criticism. A negative and distorted self-view.	Sense of Self	A diminished sense of self, but not necessarily negative. More of a fading or erasure of self-identity.
Characterized by rumination on negative thoughts, difficulty concentrating, and indecisiveness.	Cognitive Function	A quieted mind with reduced internal chatter. Disengagement from deep or complex thought.
Pain comes from the presence of intense negative feelings and self-critical thoughts.	Source of Pain	The 'pain' comes from the absence of feeling, meaning, and connection. A functional emptiness.
Can include significant changes in sleep and appetite, fatigue, and unexplained physical aches.	Physical Symptoms	General low energy and lethargy, but typically without the acute physical symptoms of depression.
Marked by a sense of hopelessness and a bleak, pessimistic view of the future.	Hope & Future	The future is not seen as hopeless, but as irrelevant. A lack of orientation towards the future.

TREATING DEPRESSION

The treatment of clinical depression is a comprehensive process aimed at restoring neurochemical balance and rebuilding healthy cognitive and behavioral patterns. Because of its complex nature, a multi-faceted approach is almost always required.

This often includes psychotherapy, where an individual can address the underlying thoughts, feelings, and life situations contributing to their depressive state. Cognitive Behavioral Therapy (CBT), for example, is highly effective in helping people reframe negative thought patterns.

In many cases, this is combined with antidepressant medication prescribed by a physician or psychiatrist. These medications are not "happy pills," but sophisticated tools designed to correct chemical imbalances in the brain, creating the stability needed for therapeutic work to be effective.

This combined approach of therapy and, when appropriate, medication is the gold standard for helping individuals lift the weight of depression and reconnect with a life of meaning and engagement.

Now, consider where anxiety disorders fit and how nulling out differs.

ANXIETY DISORDERS: WHEN EVERYTHING FEELS DANGEROUS VS. WHEN NOTHING FEELS IMPORTANT

An anxiety disorder is a state of hyper-arousal, as if the mind's accelerator is stuck to the floor. This can create a cascade of both mental and physical symptoms. The mind is filled with racing thoughts and excessive worrying, making it nearly impossible to relax or feel at ease. This constant state of high alert puts the body on uneasy footing, leading to physical responses such as a rapid heartbeat, sweating, and trembling.

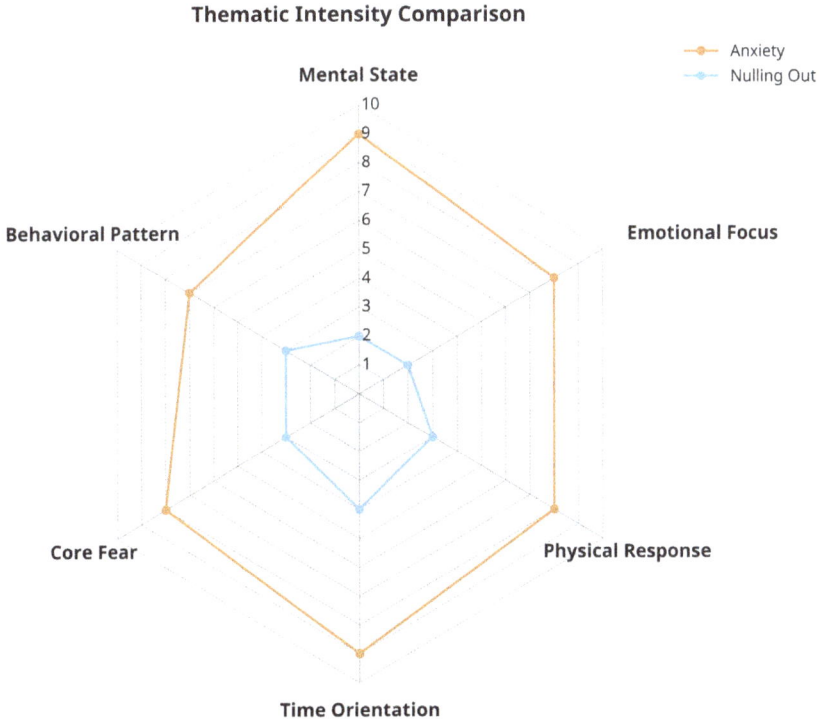

Thematic Intensity Comparison

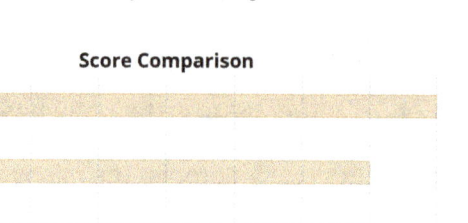

Score Comparison

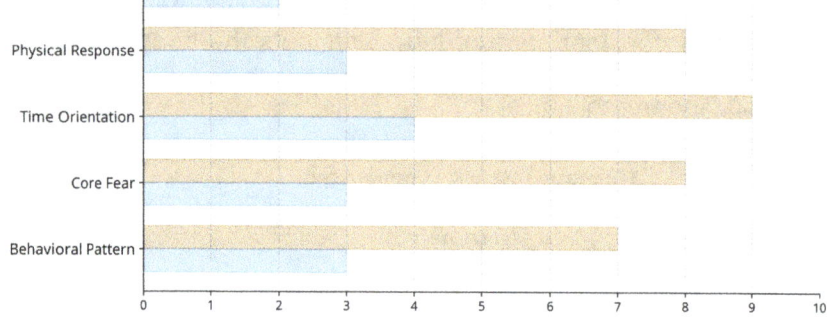

These charts visualize the profound difference in internal 'volume.' Anxiety is a state of maximum intensity—a 'loud,' hyper-aroused experience across every metric. In contrast, the nulled-out state is defined by the near-total absence of that signal, creating a state of unnerving quiet.

To cope with these symptoms, an individual will often go to great lengths to avoid any situation that might provoke their anxiety, often appearing visibly distressed. Sleep becomes elusive as their mind refuses to shut down, trapping them in a cycle of worry and exhaustion.

The core distinction lies in the internal "volume." Anxiety is a state of deafening mental and physical noise—racing thoughts, a pounding heart, a constant scan for threats. Nulling out is a state of profound, unnerving silence. This is perfectly illustrated by a simple example: an anxious person worries obsessively about whether they gave a good presentation, while a nulled-out person gives an excellent presentation and genuinely doesn't care how it was received.

Understanding that anxiety is a disorder of "too much" is the key to treatment, which is focused on restoring a sense of safety and quiet to the mind and body.

Anxiety	Aspect	Nulling Out
A state of high alert and racing thoughts. The mind is 'loud,' filled with 'what if' scenarios and worries.	Mental State	A state of mental quiet and stillness. The mind is 'quiet,' with a significant reduction in internal chatter.
Dominated by fear, dread, and a sense of impending doom. A feeling of being constantly on edge.	Emotional Focus	Characterized by a lack of emotion, including fear and worry. A state of deep apathy and numbness.
Activates the 'fight or flight' response: increased heart rate, shortness of breath, muscle tension.	Physical Response	A state of low arousal. The body is calm, sometimes to the point of lethargy. The opposite of 'fight or flight.'
Intensely focused on the future and potential negative outcomes. Constant anticipation of threats.	Time Orientation	Disconnected from a strong sense of past, present, or future. Time feels flat and irrelevant.
The fear of losing control, of being unable to cope with future events, or of something terrible happening.	Core Fear	Not driven by fear. It is a state beyond fear, where even the energy for fear is absent.
Leads to avoidance of feared situations, safety-seeking behaviors, and constant reassurance seeking.	Behavioral Pattern	Leads to passive disengagement from life's challenges and opportunities. A pattern of non-action.

TREATING ANXIETY: CALMING THE SYSTEM

Effective treatment for anxiety disorders is centered on calming a hyper-aroused nervous system and retraining the brain's response to perceived threats. The goal is to turn down the volume on the internal "false alarm" and restore a sense of psychological safety.

Once again, a cornerstone of treatment is psychotherapy, particularly evidence-based modalities like Cognitive Behavioral Therapy. CBT provides practical tools for identifying, challenging, and reframing the catastrophic thought patterns that fuel the cycle of worry and avoidance.

This is often paired with somatic and mindfulness-based techniques. Practices such as deep breathing, progressive muscle relaxation, and meditation are not just for relaxation; they are powerful skills that help an individual regulate their physiological response to anxiety.

In some cases, medication may also be used to help regulate the underlying neurochemistry, providing the stability needed for the therapeutic work to take hold.

MIDLIFE CRISIS: WHEN TIME FEELS LIMITED VS. WHEN TIME FEELS MEANINGLESS

A midlife crisis is not a slow fade; it is a sudden, internal earthquake. It's often a jarring confrontation with mortality, a heightened awareness of time running out that triggers the urgent desire for change. This is a state of intense emotional engagement, manifesting as a sudden and profound questioning of one's entire life—career choices, relationships, achievements, and more.

This internal reckoning often sparks external changes in behavior or appearance, driven by a powerful desire to recapture lost youth or finally pursue long-abandoned dreams. At its core, a midlife crisis is defined by a passionate, almost desperate search for what has been missed or wasted, and is often guided by a surprisingly clear sense of what would make life feel meaningful again.

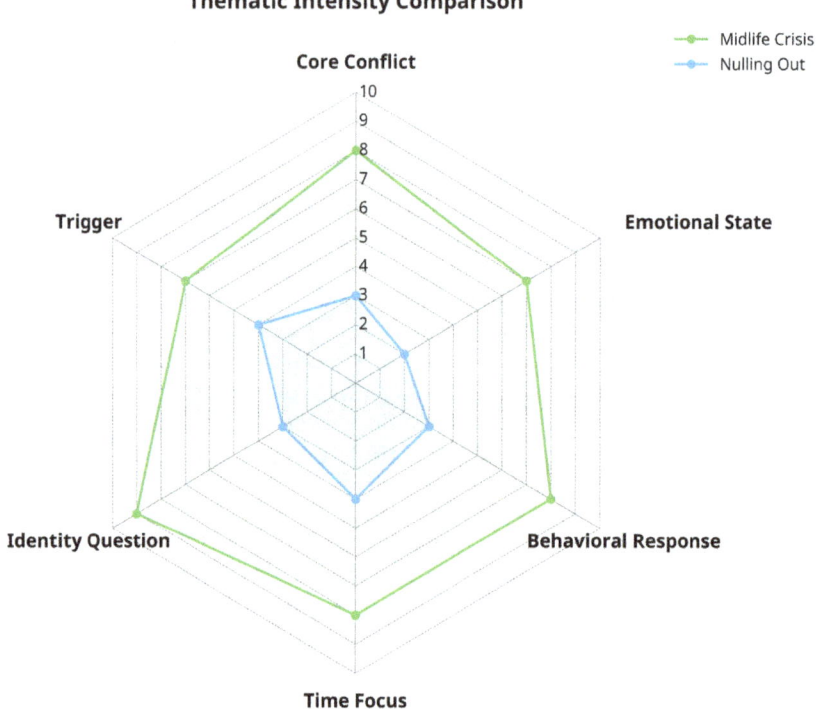

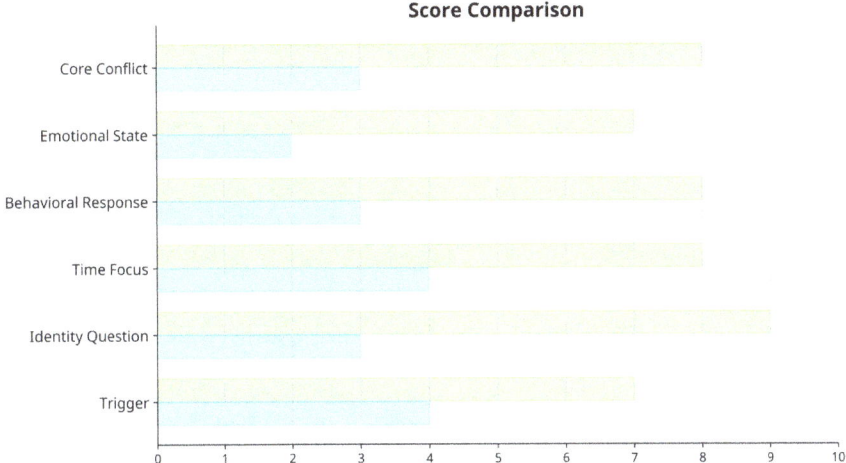

The charts above illustrate the powerful divergence between the two states. Note the high intensity of the Core Conflict, Emotional State, and Identity Question in a Midlife Crisis, versus the profound lack of intensity in the nulled-out state.

A person in a midlife crisis may buy a sports car and leave their job to pursue their passion. For all its turmoil, a midlife crisis is a profound call to action. It is an urgent, if sometimes clumsy, attempt to reclaim a life of meaning, often through dramatic changes in behavior, career, or relationships. It is a passionate, desperate search for a more authentic existence. This powerful internal reckoning is the engine driving the often-visible changes in a person's life and choices.

Midlife Crisis	Aspect	Nulling Out
A desperate search for meaning and youthfulness. A feeling that time is running out and a desire to recapture a lost self.	Core Conflict	An absence of conflict and desire. A quiet acceptance of a functional, meaningless existence.
Characterized by frustration, boredom with life, a sense of entrapment, and a desire for change and excitement.	Emotional State	Dominated by apathy and emotional numbness. A lack of both frustration and excitement.
Often leads to impulsive, dramatic changes: buying a sports car, changing careers, ending a marriage. A search for external validation.	Behavioral Response	Leads to passive disengagement and a lack of significant life changes. A pattern of quiet continuity and non-action.
Intense focus on the past (regret) and the future (making up for lost time). A rejection of the present.	Time Focus	Largely disconnected from a strong sense of time. The past, present, and future feel indistinct and irrelevant.
Asks 'Is this all there is?' and 'Who have I become?' A frantic attempt to redefine the self.	Identity Question	The question of identity is not asked. The self feels diminished or erased, not in need of redefinition.
Triggered by awareness of mortality, aging, and a sense of stagnation in career or personal life.	Trigger	Develops gradually from chronic overwhelm, not a specific midlife trigger. It is a slow fade, not a crisis.

Because this crisis is fundamentally an active search for a better path, the most effective treatments focus on helping the individual to wisely and safely complete the journey of self-discovery they have already begun, to explore their questions honestly, and to channel their desire for change into conscious, constructive, and sustainable life choices.

The search for meaning is a core part of the human journey. But when that search is abandoned altogether, it can lead to a profound spiritual emptiness, a condition with its own unique fingerprint.

SPIRITUAL EMPTINESS: WHEN GOD GOES MISSING VS. WHEN YOU GO MISSING

Spiritual emptiness is the feeling of losing connection to something larger than yourself. It's feeling cut off from any sense of higher purpose or a divine presence you once felt. It is marked by a deep yearning to reconnect, driven by the pain of feeling spiritually lost or abandoned.

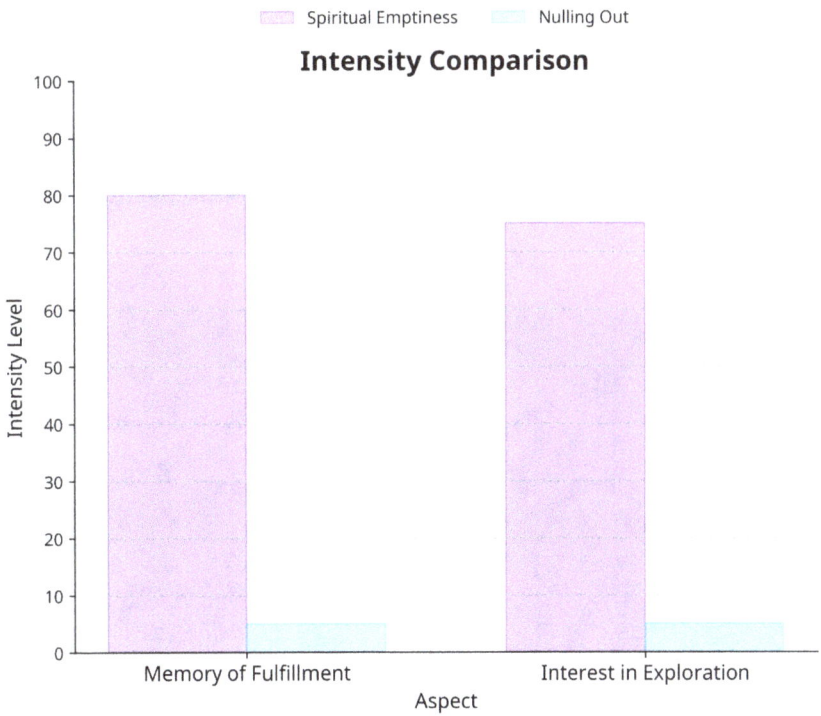

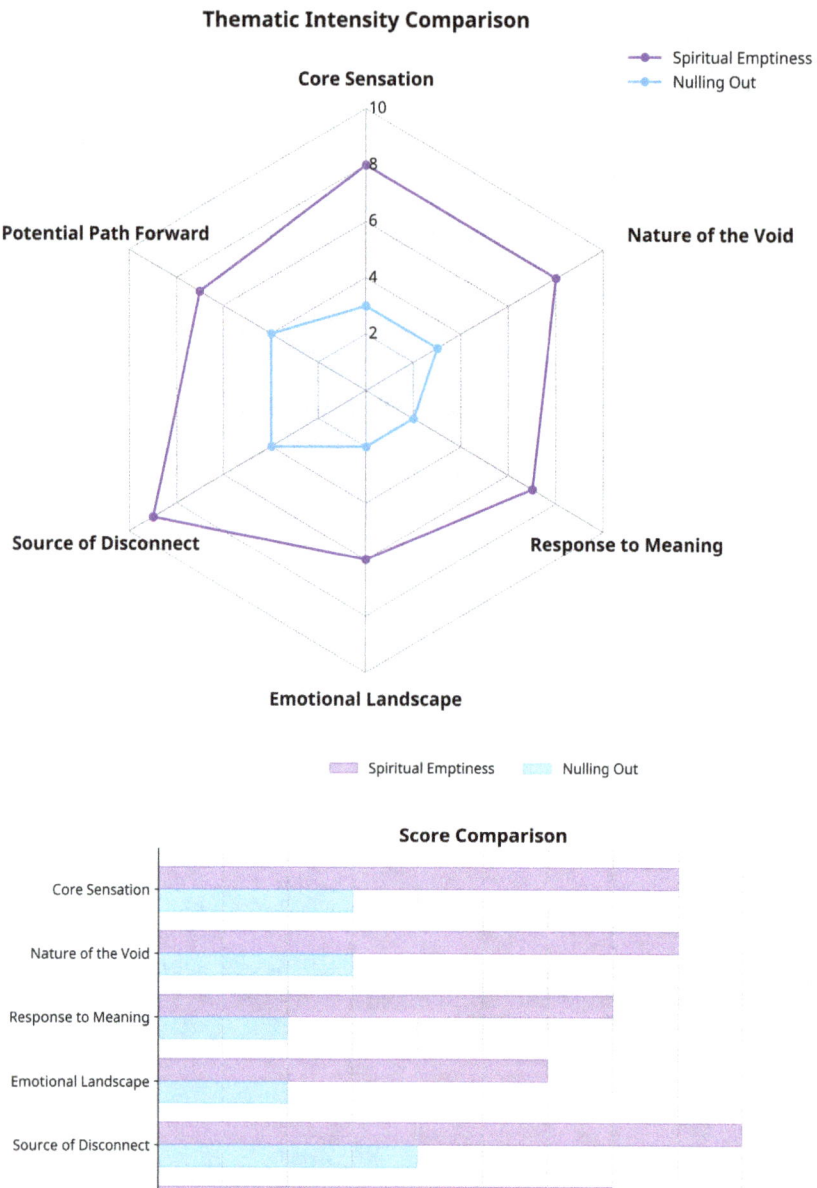

The charts above tell a layered story. The first highlights the core distinction: *Spiritual Emptiness is defined by a strong memory of fulfillment and a high interest in exploration, while the nulled-out state shows a near-total absence of both.*

The radar chart shows the overall energetic signature of this difference, and the final bar chart provides the detailed, metric-by-metric breakdown of this profound spiritual divergence.

A person in this state often has a clear memory of what spiritual fulfillment once felt like; that memory creates a deep yearning for its return. This emotional search often involves questioning long-held religious or philosophical beliefs and exploring different spiritual paths. While they may feel alone in the universe, their sense of self remains distinct and intact, defined by the very ache it feels for the transcendent connection it has lost. They clearly remember what it felt like to be "tuned in," and their interest in exploring new spiritual paths is a direct attempt to find that signal once again.

Spiritual emptiness is an ache for the transcendent. It is the feeling of a compass needle that knows "north" exists but can no longer find it. This manifests as a conscious search for connection, whether through returning to old traditions, exploring new philosophies, or engaging in contemplative practices.

Spiritual Emptiness	Aspect	Nulling Out
A feeling of being disconnected from a higher purpose, the universe, or a sense of the sacred. A 'hole in the soul.'	Core Sensation	A feeling of being disconnected from the self. A functional void where even the desire for connection is absent.
The void is perceived as a lack of connection to something larger than the self. It is a spiritual or transcendent void.	Nature of the Void	The void is a lack of internal data: emotions, strong thoughts, desires. It is a psychological and emotional void.
An active or passive yearning for meaning, purpose, and connection. A search for 'something more.'	Response to Meaning	Meaning and purpose are not sought because they feel irrelevant. The drive for meaning itself is offline.
Can involve feelings of loneliness, longing, and a sense of being adrift, but not necessarily clinical depression.	Emotional Landscape	Dominated by apathy and numbness. A flatline where longing and loneliness are also muted or absent.
A disconnect from one's inner spirit, values, or a sense of belonging in the cosmos.	Source of Disconnect	A disconnect from one's own emotional and cognitive processes. A functional self-estrangement.
Often leads to a spiritual quest, exploring religion, philosophy, meditation, or nature to find a new connection.	Potential Path Forward	The path forward requires reigniting the basic systems of emotion and cognition before a spiritual quest is even possible.

The journey is defined by this active yearning. Therefore, the path forward is not one of treatment, but of guided, personal exploration to help the individual reconnect with their own sense of the sacred.

While spiritual emptiness is a quiet ache for a lost connection, an existential crisis is a much louder and more fundamental questioning of reality itself. Let's examine this profound condition next.

EXISTENTIAL CRISIS: WHEN LIFE'S MEANING IS QUESTIONED VS. WHEN MEANING NO LONGER MATTERS

An existential crisis is the experience of becoming unmoored, the feeling that the map of life might be meaningless. It is a profound and often distressing confrontation with the fundamental questions of existence: Why am I here? What is my purpose? What is the point of it all? The anchors of previously held beliefs and assumptions are suddenly gone, leaving one adrift on a sea of profound questions.

This is an intensely active and often tumultuous state, characterized by deep questions about life's purpose and one's personal significance in the universe. It involves a serious wrestling with the big three: your mortality, your freedom, and your responsibility for your own choices. It is a state of heightened awareness, where every choice and its consequence feel monumental.

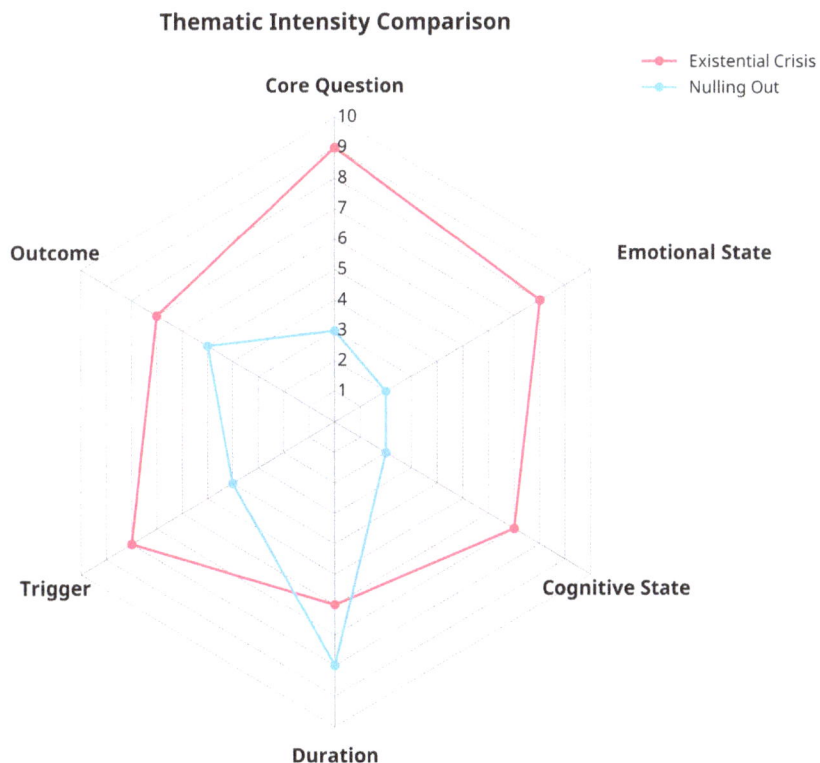

Thematic Intensity Comparison

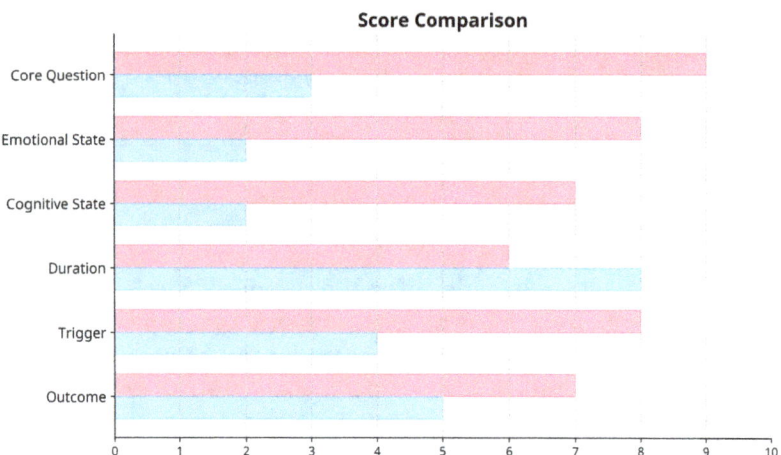

The charts above illustrate the key diagnostic differences. Note the intense emotional and cognitive engagement of an Existential Crisis versus the profound disengagement of the nulled-out state

This is a state of deep emotional distress about the potential for meaninglessness, which fuels an active search for philosophical answers. It is a period of deep thinking, a heightened awareness of every choice, and a fundamental quest to define what, in the end, makes a life worth living.

The emotional distress comes directly from the weight of these questions. Because this is a crisis of meaning, not of malfunction, the path forward is not just about treatment, but about a courageous exploration of these ultimate concerns to forge a newly defined sense of purpose. In doing so, with every question, more questions arise coupled with doubts about the questions themselves and the answers they might propose.

Aspect	Existential Crisis	Nulling Out
Core Question	Questions the very meaning and purpose of life, existence, and one's place in the universe. Asks 'Why am I here?'	Not a question, but a state of being where purpose feels irrelevant. A functional void rather than an active search.
Emotional State	Dominated by anxiety, dread, a sense of absurdity, and feeling lost in a meaningless cosmos.	Characterized by profound apathy, emotional numbness, and a lack of both positive and negative feelings. A flatline.
Cognitive State	Intense philosophical rumination, questioning fundamental beliefs, searching for answers to unanswerable questions.	Marked by a quiet mind, reduced internal chatter, and a disengagement from deep thought or worry. Mental stillness.
Duration	Can be a prolonged period, often recurring at major life transitions, but is typically a phase.	Often a long-term, chronic state that can last for years, becoming a baseline state of being.
Trigger	Often triggered by major life events (death, career change), confronting mortality, or realizing the universe's indifference.	Develops gradually from prolonged stress, burnout, or as a defense mechanism against overwhelming input. Less about a single event.
Outcome	Can lead to a new, self-defined sense of purpose, deeper self-awareness, or conversely, despair and nihilism.	Leads to a state of functional non-engagement, detachment from personal and professional life, and a quiet erosion of self.

WHY THESE DISTINCTIONS ARE IMPORTANT: THE TREATMENT QUAGMIRE

We have now drawn a clear line in the sand between six familiar conditions and the unique fingerprint of nulling out. Making these distinctions is not an academic exercise; it is a crucial and often life-saving act because getting the diagnosis wrong can cause real harm.

When a doctor treats burnout with rest, a therapist treats anxiety with calming techniques, or a psychiatrist treats depression with medication, they are applying the correct solutions to the correctly identified problems.

But when those same correct solutions are applied to a nulled-out individual, they are not only ineffective, they can be dangerous. They can reinforce the disconnection, deepen the emptiness, and validate the terrifying internal belief that one is fundamentally broken beyond repair; this is the treatment quagmire. And it is the reason that understanding the true nature of nulling out is the first, essential step on the path back to being fully alive.

WHAT REALLY WORKS: RECONNECTION

The diagnosis is clear. The confusion, the emptiness, the profound sense of disconnection—this is not burnout, nor is it depression, nor is it a crisis of meaning. It has a name: nulling out.

And here is the most important truth: You are not broken. Your true self is not damaged, but merely dormant. Your emotions are not gone, just temporarily disconnected. You're living behind a veil that has obscured what it feels like to be vibrantly alive.

You do not need to be fixed. You just need to reconnect.

Having a correct diagnosis is the first and most critical step. Now that you understand the true nature of the problem, the entire second half of this book will be dedicated to the solution: a practical, step-by-step framework for the art and science of reconnection.

THE CRITICAL QUESTION

The journey through the preceding chapters raises the most important question for anyone who sees themselves in these pages: If nulling out isn't depression, burnout, or any other condition we currently recognize, how exactly does it happen?

How does a lively, creative, authentic individual become emotionally empty?

How do qualities essential for success—discipline, curiosity, adaptability, a strong drive for excellence—lead to a profound disconnection from one's true self?

Understanding this process is crucial, because you can't undo what you don't understand. And more importantly, recognizing how nulling out develops will help you see that every step that led away from yourself can be retraced.

In the next section of this book, we will explore exactly how high achievers lose themselves in success through thousands of tiny optimizations that gradually erase the person while perfecting the performance.

The path that led you away from yourself is also the path that can lead you back.

PART II
THE
DESCENT

*"A soul doesn't shatter all at once. It fades, one
rewarded compromise at a time."*

CHAPTER 4
HOW HIGH ACHIEVERS LOSE THEMSELVES

"Most people are other people. Their thoughts are someone else's opinions, their lives a mimicry."

Oscar Wilde

It starts with a single moment of recognition: the behavior that gets rewarded versus the behavior that feels authentic.

Jeffrey was twenty-five when he first noticed it. Fresh out of his MBA program and six months into what he considered his dream job at a prestigious consulting firm, he found himself in a client meeting where his instinct was to ask probing questions about the human impact of the proposed restructuring.

But he hesitated. He'd been watching his colleagues, and the ones who got promoted asked different kinds of questions—questions about efficiency metrics, cost savings, and implementation timelines. Questions that showed they were focused on the client's bottom line, not the employees who would be affected. He worried about what would happen if he challenged the status quo, what would happen if he deviated from what seemed to be the most essential aspect of business—money.

So, he asked the "right" questions instead.

The meeting went well; his manager complimented his focus, and the client appreciated his practical approach. Jeffrey was assigned to the next high-profile project.

But something inside him stilled. He had thrown out his personal standards as he padded his bank account. At first, it seemed necessary. It's a dog-eat-dog world, he thought. The silence spread through his veins until the voice that told him to pause was drowned out.

It was such a small moment, barely noticeable at all—a minor course correction in professional behavior, the kind of adaptation that successful people make dozens of times as they learn to navigate their careers effectively.

Jeffrey didn't know it at the time, but he had just taken the first step toward nulling out.

THE OPTIMIZATION TRAP

High achievers become nulled-out through a process that feels like growth but is actually systematic self-erasure. It begins with a perfectly reasonable understanding: Certain responses get rewarded while others do not. Certain versions of yourself are more valuable in professional contexts than others.

Recognizing this isn't wrong. Jeffrey was right to notice that asking about human impact wasn't what his firm valued. A creative professional is right to notice that their most innovative ideas aren't what their clients want to pay for. An empathetic leader is right to observe that their instinct to prioritize people over profits isn't what gets them promoted.

The problem isn't the recognition—it's what happens next.

THE GRADUAL PROCESS OF SELF-EDITING

Once you recognize which version of yourself gets rewarded, optimization becomes inevitable. High achievers are natural optimizers; it's part of what makes them successful. They see a system, identify what works within it, and adapt accordingly.

So, Jeffrey began to edit himself in real time. Before speaking in meetings, he runs a quick internal filter: Will this comment advance the business objectives? Does this question demonstrate strategic thinking? Is this the kind of insight that gets noticed and valued?

The unfiltered responses—human concerns, ethical questions, creative tangents—don't disappear immediately. They just get marked as "inappropriate for this context" and filed away for later consideration.

The only problem is that later consideration never comes. Every context becomes a professional context, and every professional context rewards the same optimized version of himself.

THE EXPANSION EFFECT

What started as situational adaptation quickly expanded beyond the original context. Jeffrey found himself filtering not just in client meetings, but in team meetings, casual conversations with colleagues, and networking events. The optimized professional version had become the default version because it's safer, more effective, and consistently rewarded.

Soon, he was filtering at dinner parties with other professionals. Then, in conversations with his family, when they asked about work. Then, in internal conversations with himself as he planned his career moves.

The optimized self isn't just a mask he put on for work; it has become the operating system running his entire life.

THE REINFORCEMENT CYCLE

Each success achieved through optimization reinforces the process. Jeffrey got promoted. His income increased. His colleagues respected his strategic thinking. His family was proud of his achievements. Every external indicator suggested that the optimization was working perfectly.

And it was working—for external metrics. His performance reviews were excellent. His client satisfaction scores were high. His career trajectory was exactly what he'd planned.

But with each reward, the unoptimized version of himself got pushed further into the background. The parts of him that cared about things other than business objectives became less accessible, not because they were damaged, but because they were consistently marked as irrelevant.

THE SYSTEMATIC SUPPRESSION OF THE AUTHENTIC SELF

The most insidious part of this process is how natural it feels. Jeffrey wasn't deliberately trying to erase himself—he was trying to become more effective, more professional, more successful. Each time he chose the optimized response over the authentic one, it felt like growth.

Now, his authentic impulses don't fight back dramatically. They don't stage a rebellion or create obvious internal conflict. They simply fade, like a radio signal moving out of range.

When Jeffrey first started filtering his responses, he could still access his unoptimized thoughts and feelings. He knew what he really thought about the restructuring proposal; he just chose not to voice it. He was aware of his empathetic concerns; he simply decided they weren't appropriate for the business context.

But consciousness requires attention, and attention requires energy. After months of marking certain thoughts as irrelevant, Jeffrey stopped generating them as readily. After years of dismissing certain emotional responses as unprofessional, he stopped having them automatically.

The authentic self doesn't die—it just goes dormant. Like a muscle that atrophies from lack of use, the capacity for unfiltered responses gradually weakens until it's barely perceptible.

THE EFFICIENCY ADDICTION

High achievers become addicted to the efficiency of optimization. Making decisions becomes faster when you don't have to process multiple conflicting impulses, such as considering the impact on human performance or morale. Social interactions become smoother when you're not wrestling with complex, authentic responses. Professional advancement becomes more predictable when you're not distracted by concerns that do not directly serve your and the client's objectives.

Jeffrey discovered that the optimized version of himself was remarkably efficient. He could walk into any professional situation and immediately know what was expected, what would be valued, and how to position himself for success. He didn't need to waste time on internal debates or struggle with ethical concerns about the implications. His optimized self ran like a well-oiled machine—smooth, predictable, and highly effective.

But machines don't have preferences. They don't get excited about possibilities or feel conflicted about trade-offs. They simply execute their programming efficiently.

THE MOMENT OF RECOGNITION

Twelve years into his career, Jeffrey sat in his corner office, looking at his latest performance review:

"Exceptional strategic thinking."

"Consistently exceeds client expectations."

"Ready for senior leadership roles."

He should have felt proud. He should have felt accomplished. He should have felt excited about the trajectory he'd created.

Instead, he feels nothing. Not sad, not disappointed, not even particularly concerned. Just ... empty. Like he's reading someone else's performance review for someone else's career.

THE CONTAMINATION OF PERSONAL LIFE

The optimization that begins in professional contexts doesn't stay contained there. Jeffrey discovered that the efficient, filtered version of himself works well in other areas, too.

At family gatherings, he learned to give the responses that create the least friction. When his mother asks about his love life, Jeffrey provides updates that sound appropriately successful without revealing his actual confusion about what he wants in a relationship. When his father asks about his career, he shares achievements that make him proud rather than his own growing sense of disconnection from the work itself.

In romantic relationships, he's become skilled at being the kind of partner that works well on paper. He's supportive without being needy, ambitious without being threatening, independent without being distant. He says yes to activities that make sense for couples in their demographic, expresses preferences that align with his partner's lifestyle, and makes relationship decisions based on compatibility metrics rather than any deep emotional pull.

The optimization spreads because it's effective everywhere. Family relationships become smoother when you're not bringing up complicated feelings or inconvenient needs. Friendships are easier to maintain when you're consistently agreeable and low-maintenance. Even casual social interactions flow better when you're operating from a predictable, optimized script.

THE LOSS OF INTERNAL COMPASS

What Jeffrey doesn't realize is that his capacity to access authentic preferences is atrophying from disuse. Initially, he was making conscious choices to prioritize optimized responses over authentic ones. But after years of this pattern, authentic responses become harder and harder to locate.

When his significant other asks where he wants to go for dinner, Jeffrey genuinely doesn't know. Not because he's indecisive, but because he's lost reliable access to the part of himself that has food preferences. He can analyze which restaurant would create the best experience for both of them, determine which cuisine would be most suitable for their budget and dietary restrictions, and identify the most convenient location. But as for what he actually wants to eat? That signal has grown so faint he can barely detect it.

When friends invite him to weekend activities, he evaluates the invitation like a business decision. Which option will strengthen these relationships? Which will provide the best networking opportunities? Which will be the most Instagram-worthy? The question of which activity would actually bring him joy doesn't even occur to him anymore because joy isn't a category his decision-making process recognizes.

THE SUBSTITUTION OF METRICS FOR MEANING

As authentic internal signals fade, Jeff develops an increasingly sophisticated system of external metrics to guide his choices. He tracks his career progression against industry benchmarks. He evaluates his relationships based on compatibility assessments and mutual benefits. He measures his lifestyle against social media representations of success.

These metrics work remarkably well for creating a life that looks successful from the outside. Jeff's apartment is beautiful, his job is prestigious, his relationship appears stable, his social life seems active and well-rounded.

But metrics can't generate meaning. They can optimize for outcomes, but they can't create the internal satisfaction that comes from choices that align with authentic desires.

THE POINT OF COMPLETE DISCONNECTION

Fourteen years into this process, Jeffrey had reached what felt to him like the pinnacle of optimization. He'd been promoted to senior management. His salary had tripled since graduation. He lived in a beautiful apartment in the right neighborhood, was dating an accomplished professional who looked good on his arm and perfect on paper, and he maintained friendships with other successful people who enhanced his social capital.

He'd become extraordinarily efficient at living. Every decision gets filtered through his well-developed system of metrics, every response gets optimized for maximum effectiveness, and every interaction serves multiple strategic purposes.

But somewhere in this perfect efficiency, Jeffrey has disappeared entirely.

The moment he realized this was unremarkable in its ordinariness. He was sitting in his favorite restaurant—actually, the restaurant that made the most sense given its location, price point, and menu options that accommodated his partner's dietary restrictions. He was eating food that was nutritionally optimal and Instagram-worthy. He was having a conversation about topics that are appropriately engaging but not controversial.

Out of nowhere, he realized he couldn't remember the last time he wanted anything.

Not that he couldn't have something he wanted—he couldn't remember actually wanting anything at all. When was the last time he felt excited about a possibility? When did he last feel drawn to an experience for no practical reason? When was the last time he made a choice based purely on desire rather than optimization?

He couldn't access the answers because the capacity to want things—really want them, not just recognize that they would be beneficial—had gone completely offline.

THE HIGH-FUNCTIONING VOID

This is where Jeffrey became truly nulled-out. He continued to perform at an exceptional level. His work was still excellent, his relationships still stable, his life still enviable by external standards. But he was now operating entirely as an automation, a sophisticated program running smoothly without an authentic operator at the controls.

He goes through his days making decisions, but they're not really his decision; they're the logical outputs of the optimization system he's built. He has conversations, but they're not really his conversations; they're the predictable interactions that his social programming generates. He experiences achievements, but they're not really his achievements; they're just the inevitable results of efficient execution.

The most disturbing part isn't that he feels bad about this; the most disturbing part is that he doesn't feel anything about it. The capacity to care has been optimized away along with everything else.

THE INVISIBLE SUCCESS STORY

From the outside, Jeffrey appears to be thriving. Colleagues admire his composure and strategic thinking. Friends see him as someone who has his life together. Family members point to him as an example of what successful professionals look like.

No one realizes that the person they think they're admiring has essentially ceased to exist. They're looking at an extremely sophisticated performance with no performer behind it.

THE UNIVERSAL PATTERN

Jeffrey's story isn't unique—in fact, it's the template for many other people. Across industries, personality types, and life circumstances, high achievers follow remarkably similar paths to nulling out.

Bryon, a software engineer, suppresses his creative impulses because the startup world rewards efficiency over innovation. Donald, a physician, suppresses his empathetic responses because the medical system values speed and accuracy over patient connection. Blane, an attorney, filters out his ethical concerns because the legal profession rewards winning over justice. Sheldon, an accountant, loses his moral compass because clients value tax savings over honesty.

Each follows the same progression: recognition of what gets rewarded, systematic optimization toward those rewards, gradual suppression of non-optimized responses, and eventual disconnection from authentic self-direction.

The specific triggers vary—different industries reward different types of optimizations—but the mechanism remains constant. High achievers, by definition, are good at identifying success patterns and adapting to them. This very skill becomes the instrument of their own erasure.

THE ACCELERATION EFFECT

What makes this process particularly dangerous for high achievers is how quickly it accelerates once it begins. Unlike people who struggle professionally, high achievers get immediate and consistent reinforcement for their optimization efforts.

Every promotion, salary increase, and moment of professional recognition validates the choice to prioritize optimized responses over authentic ones. Every networking success, relationship milestone, and lifestyle upgrade further confirms that the system is working perfectly.

This creates a feedback loop that makes it nearly impossible to recognize what's being lost. When optimization is continuously rewarded, questioning the process feels not just ungrateful but irrational.

Jeffrey's colleagues who seem less successful often maintain stronger connections to their authentic selves precisely because they haven't received the constant external validation that would encourage complete optimization. Their "failures" to fully adapt to professional expectations accidentally preserve the parts of themselves that Jeffrey optimized away.

THE COMPOUND EFFECT

Like compound interest, the effects of optimization accumulate over time in ways that aren't immediately apparent. Suppressing one authentic response makes it easier to suppress the next one. Optimizing one area of life makes optimization feel natural in other areas. Success achieved through filtering authentic impulses makes those impulses increasingly irrelevant.

After several years, the nulled-out individual isn't making conscious choices to suppress authenticity—authenticity has simply become inaccessible. They're not deciding to prioritize optimization over genuine preference; genuine preference has already faded to the point where it's no longer a factor in decision-making. It's no longer an option because it's invisible, a ghost with no voice.

WHY THE PATTERN IS NEARLY IMPOSSIBLE TO INTERRUPT

The most insidious aspect of this progression is that every external indicator suggests it's working perfectly. Unlike addiction, mental illness, or other problems that create obvious negative consequences, nulling out creates increasingly positive external outcomes while destroying internal life.

Jeffrey's bank account has grown larger, but his sense of self has grown smaller. His professional reputation has strengthened as his personal identity weakened. His life has become more impressive to others but less meaningful to himself.

Jeffrey and others like him have inadvertently created a unique form of cognitive dissonance. When someone feels empty, but their life looks fulfilled, the natural conclusion is that the emptiness must be indicative of deeper personal problems. They're ungrateful, selfish, overly ambitious, maybe thoughtless or inconsiderate and cold. The idea that the success itself might be causing the emptiness feels counterintuitive because they're not actually ungrateful.

Still, they feel empty and can't put their finger on why. The missing link in their seemingly successful life is the life they left behind.

THE GRATITUDE TRAP

Well-meaning friends, family members, and even therapists often reinforce the nulling out process by emphasizing gratitude.

"Look at everything you've accomplished!"

"Think about how many people would love to have your problems!"

"You should feel proud of what you've achieved!"

Gratitude for external circumstances can't fill an internal void, and appreciating your success won't reconnect you to your authentic self. Likewise, being thankful for your opportunities won't restore your capacity to feel genuine excitement about possibilities.

So, on top of feeling empty, Jeffrey now feels guilty about his emptiness. Now he's not just disconnected from himself—he's also ashamed of that disconnection. This drives him to optimize even harder to prove that he really is grateful for his good fortune.

THE COMPARISON ILLUSION

High achievers also struggle to recognize their nulling out because they're surrounded by other high achievers who appear to be thriving. Jeffrey looks around his professional and social circles and sees other people who seem to be successfully balancing achievement with satisfaction.

What he doesn't realize is that many of them are nulled-out, too— they've just become skilled at performing "to satisfaction" along with everything else. The networking events, social media posts, and casual conversations are full of people who have optimized their presentation of contentment while experiencing the same internal void.

The rare individuals who have maintained an authentic connection to themselves often appear less successful by conventional metrics, which reinforces the false belief that authenticity and achievement are incompatible.

THE SUNK COST FALLACY

Perhaps most powerfully, the years invested in optimization create enormous psychological pressure to continue the process. Jeffrey has spent over a decade building this career, this lifestyle, this version of himself. The idea that it might all be fundamentally misaligned with who he actually is feels too overwhelming to seriously consider.

Starting over would mean admitting that years of "growth" were actually years of self-erasure. It would mean questioning not just current choices but the entire trajectory that brought him to this point. It would mean disappointing people who are proud of his achievements and potentially losing the financial security and social status he's worked so hard to build.

So he continues optimizing, hoping that the next promotion, relationship milestone, or lifestyle upgrade will finally generate the satisfaction that's been missing.

THE CRISIS THAT BREAKS THROUGH

For some nulled-out individuals, the pattern continues indefinitely. They live their entire lives as optimized performances, never reconnecting with their authentic selves, never experiencing the satisfaction that comes from choices aligned with genuine desire.

But for others, something eventually breaks through the numbness. Not a dramatic breakdown—nulled-out people rarely have dramatic breakdowns because they've lost the capacity for dramatic responses. Instead, it's usually a moment of such profound disconnection that even their optimized system can't explain it away.

For Jeffrey, it happened on what should have been one of the best days of his life. He'd just received a promotion to vice president—the goal he'd been working toward for three years. The salary increase was substantial. The responsibility was exactly what he wanted. The recognition from senior leadership validated everything he'd worked for.

He sat in his new office, looking at the congratulatory emails flooding his inbox, and realized he felt absolutely nothing. Not relief, not pride, not excitement about the challenges ahead. Just a vast, echoing emptiness where satisfaction should have been.

But this time, instead of dismissing the feeling or trying to manufacture appropriate emotions, something in him recognized the emptiness as a problem worth paying attention to. Maybe it was because he'd achieved the goal he thought would fix everything, and it hadn't. Maybe it was because the disconnection had become so complete that even his optimization system recognized something was wrong.

Whatever triggered it, Jeffrey had his first authentic response in years: the genuine recognition that something was fundamentally wrong with his life, despite how successful it appeared.

THE DANGEROUS AWAKENING

This moment of recognition is both hopeful and dangerous. Hopeful because it's the first authentic response Jeff has had in years—proof that the capacity for genuine feeling still exists somewhere inside him. Dangerous because awakening to the void without understanding what caused it or how to fill it can lead to destructive attempts to feel something, anything.

Some nulled-out individuals respond to this recognition by making dramatic changes—leaving jobs, ending relationships, moving to different cities—hoping that external changes will restore internal connection. But because the problem isn't with their circumstances but with their disconnection from themselves, these changes rarely help and often create additional chaos.

Others respond by escalating their attempts to feel something real. The affair, the reckless investment, the substance abuse, the extreme risk-taking—these aren't random self-destructive behaviors. They're desperate attempts by people who feel nothing to feel something, even if that something is pain, danger, or chaos.

THE RECOGNITION POINT

The moment when a nulled-out individual first recognizes their condition is crucial. With the right understanding and approach, it can become the turning point toward reconnection and recovery. Without proper understanding, it can lead to years of misguided attempts to solve the wrong problem.

Jeffrey was lucky. Instead of making dramatic external changes or escalating into dangerous behaviors, he began to research what might be happening to him. He discovered that what he was experiencing had a name and a path forward.

He learned that he's not broken, ungrateful, or having a midlife crisis. He's nulled-out. And nulling out, unlike many conditions that affect achievers, is completely reversible.

THE HOPE IN RECOGNITION

Jeffrey's moment of recognition—the authentic acknowledgment that something is fundamentally wrong despite his external success—represents the most important step in reversing the nulling out process. You can't reconnect with something until you recognize that you've been disconnected from it.

This recognition is itself proof that the authentic self hasn't been destroyed, only suppressed. The capacity to feel genuine concern over the emptiness, to have an authentic response to the disconnection, demonstrates that the person underneath the optimization is still there, just waiting to be brought back online.

Tragically, most nulled-out individuals never reach this point of recognition. They continue optimizing indefinitely, mistaking efficiency for fulfillment, performance for satisfaction, and external validation for internal peace. They live their lives as sophisticated programs running smoothly without an authentic operator at the controls.

But those who do recognize what's happened to them have a clear path forward. Unlike depression, which can involve chemical imbalances, or anxiety, which may require ongoing management, nulling out is purely a problem of disconnection. The wiring is still intact; it just needs to be reconnected.

THE PROCESS REVERSAL

Every step that led Jeffrey away from himself can be retraced to lead him back. The optimization habits that disconnected him from authentic responses can be gradually replaced with practices that reconnect him to his genuine preferences. The external metrics that replaced internal signals can be supplemented with attention to authentic desires and responses.

The key is understanding that reconnection, like disconnection, happens gradually. Jeffrey didn't null out overnight, and he won't reconnect overnight. Unlike the years he spent systematically suppressing his authentic self, the reconnection process is conscious, intentional, and oriented toward wholeness rather than efficiency.

THE WARNING FOR OTHERS

Jeffrey's story serves as both a cautionary tale and a roadmap. For high achievers who recognize early signs of disconnection in themselves, it demonstrates how quickly optimization can become self-erasure when left unchecked. For those already deep in the nulling out process, it provides hope that recognition is possible and recovery is achievable.

But perhaps most importantly, it illustrates why understanding this process matters beyond individual recovery. When our highest achievers become nulled-out, the consequences extend far beyond personal emptiness.

THE BROADER IMPLICATIONS

Nulled-out individuals don't just lose themselves; they lose the capacity to make decisions that serve anything other than optimized outcomes. They become incapable of considering the human cost of efficient choices, the ethical implications of strategic decisions, or the long-term consequences of prioritizing metrics over meaning.

When Jeffrey was fully nulled-out, he could execute brilliant business strategies without any genuine consideration of how they affected the people involved. He could optimize for client satisfaction without any authentic investment in whether the outcomes served broader human goals. He could build impressive results while being completely disconnected from whether those results contributed to anything meaningful.

This isn't because nulled-out individuals are bad people—it's because they've lost access to the parts of themselves that would consider such questions relevant.

In the next chapter, we'll explore what happens when nulled-out individuals reach their breaking point—when the emptiness becomes so unbearable that they'll do anything to feel something real, even if it destroys everything they've built.

A person who feels nothing might eventually do anything to feel something. And those desperate attempts to reconnect with authentic feeling can have devastating consequences for individuals, families, and organizations alike.

CHAPTER 5
THE WARNING SIGNS EVERYONE MISSES

"The privilege of a lifetime is being who you are."
Joseph Campbell

Joseph Campbell had it right. But I would add that the privilege of a lifetime is knowing who you are and having the freedom to be that.

The signs were there for months before Mark's life imploded, but no one recognized them—including Mark himself.

Mark was a consummate professional. He never missed deadlines, never lost his composure, and consistently delivered exceptional results. His wife saw him as a provider who paid the bills on time, maintained the household efficiently, and showed up to every family obligation without complaint. His friends and colleagues viewed him as someone who was reliable, agreeable, and impressively successful by every conventional measure.

What they all missed were the signs of a man slowly disappearing from his own life.

Mark would pause for just a beat too long when asked what he wanted for dinner because the question genuinely confused him, not because he was mulling over menu choices. He'd smile and nod during conversations, while his eyes remained completely flat, seemingly engaged with the interaction but disconnected from any genuine response. He'd agree to social plans with the same tone he used to confirm meeting times—pleasant, appropriate, somewhat monotone, and utterly devoid of actual enthusiasm.

These weren't signs of stress or burnout. Mark wasn't irritable, exhausted, or obviously struggling. If anything, he seemed more composed and efficient than ever.

But he wasn't—he was nulled-out. And nulling out has its own early warning system if you know what to look for.

The first sign is often a strange relationship with success. When Mark received the biggest bonus of his career, he felt the same mild, fleeting satisfaction he might get from completing a routine task. There was no joy, no internal celebration, just the flat acknowledgment that another box had been checked. This is the hallmark of the nulled-out state: milestones that should feel meaningful are met with nothing more than a brief sense of relief that one hasn't failed.

This emotional flatline is often mistaken for professional composure. Unlike the heavy weight of depression, there is no persistent sadness. But there is also no excitement about new opportunities, and no real anxiety about challenges. Life unfolds in a perpetual, sterile neutral.

This void forces decision-making to become algorithmic. When Mark's wife asked if he wanted to renovate the kitchen or take a vacation with the bonus money, he couldn't answer. Instead, he spent twenty minutes outlining the financial pros and cons of each, because "what appeals to me" was no longer an accessible piece of data. He could tell you what was most efficient and what was strategically sound, but he could not tell you what he *wanted*.

This autopilot extended to all of his relationships. Mark could conduct a dinner party conversation flawlessly—asking the right questions, commenting on current events, performing the role of an engaged friend—all while being completely disconnected from everyone in the room, including himself. It was a life lived from a script, a masterful performance with no one in the director's chair.

This internal algorithm soon ran his entire life. The optimization mindset that made him successful at work infiltrated his personal choices, evaluating everything for maximum benefit with minimum investment. Mark's weekends looked like a productivity consultant's dream: exercise that maximized health outcomes, social events that strengthened professional networks, and hobbies that developed marketable skills. He did nothing purely for pleasure, because "pleasure" was no longer a variable his system could compute.

This rigid optimization made anything spontaneous feel like a threat. When friends suggested an impromptu dinner at a new restaurant, Mark's first instinct wasn't excitement. It was a jolt of mild anxiety. He hadn't researched the menu, read the reviews, or confirmed the reservation system. The open-ended nature of the experience felt less like an adventure and more like a problem he couldn't control.

This eventually led to a quiet paralysis. When faced with any question about personal preference—what movie to watch, where to go on vacation—he genuinely had no answer. The reliable internal signal of his own authentic desires had grown so faint, he could no longer hear it at all.

Eventually, this disconnection spread to his own body. He began to lose awareness of its most basic cues, treating it like a machine to be maintained rather than a part of himself. He ate when the clock said 12:30, not when he felt hunger. He exercised according to an optimal schedule, not when his body craved movement. He realized he couldn't remember the last time he'd eaten something simply because it sounded delicious, rather than because it was nutritionally appropriate.

This mechanical self-care extended to every routine. Showers, grooming, even sleep, were all executed with perfect efficiency, but with no sense of pleasure or nurturing. And while he often slept a full eight hours, he never felt truly rested.

Mark was experiencing the unique, profound exhaustion that comes not from a lack of sleep, but from a life spent running sophisticated programs with no one at the controls.

This profound sense of detachment was most insidious in his social world. Mark's colleagues often commented on his excellent listening skills, never realizing his attentiveness was purely procedural. He processed their words, responded with thoughtful answers, and maintained a flawless performance, seeming like an engaged and empathetic peer, all while feeling no genuine curiosity or connection.

If you're thinking artificial intelligence, you'd be right. That was exactly how Mark was behaving. His responses were calculated, researched, and accurate, but without human emotion or nuance.

Even his closest relationships shifted into maintenance mode. He remembered every birthday, scheduled the regular check-ins, and fulfilled every social obligation with perfect reliability, but the warmth was gone. His care began to feel programmatic, not personal, like a system being maintained rather than a relationship being nurtured. His wife started to feel it first—a strange, unnerving hollowness behind the perfectly executed role of a loving husband.

And here is the most tragic irony: for Mark, this all felt surprisingly easy. Unlike introverts, who are drained by social interaction, Mark was able to navigate any party or meeting effortlessly. He could perform for hours on end precisely because he had no real emotional skin in the game. It required far less energy to run a script than it did to engage as a real, vulnerable human being.

WHY THESE SIGNS ARE SO EASY TO MISS

The most dangerous aspect of these warning signs is that they are hard to spot. They do not look like problems; they look like success.

Every sign of a person nulling out—emotional stability, efficient decision-making, consistent performance—is celebrated by our culture as a mark of maturity and good judgment. These behaviors are consistently rewarded. Mark's colleagues wanted to emulate his composure, his clients appreciated his strategic thinking, and his family benefited from his reliability. The very things that signaled his internal erasure were the things that generated external praise.

Compounding this is the fact that the condition is internally silent. Unlike anxiety or depression, which create obvious distress, nulling out operates below the threshold of conscious pain. The individual doesn't feel bad enough to seek help; they simply feel less. It is a quiet fade, not a loud crisis, making it incredibly easy to ignore until it's too late.

Mark's timeline illustrates this progression clearly.

Year 1: Occasional moments of emotional flatness after achievements, dismissed as natural adaptation to higher performance standards.

Year 2: Decision-making becomes noticeably more analytical and less intuitive, praised by colleagues as increased strategic thinking.

Year 3: Personal preferences become harder to access, leading to more efficient but less personally satisfying choices.

Year 4: Relationships shift into maintenance mode, still functional but lacking authentic engagement.

Year 5: Complete disconnection from internal signals, with all choices driven by external optimization.

By the final stage, Mark isn't just showing warning signs—he's fully nulled-out. But because the progression happened gradually, and each stage looked like an improvement over the previous one, no one recognized the trajectory until it was complete.

WHAT HAPPENS WHEN THE FADE IS COMPLETE?

What happens when a person who feels nothing can no longer tolerate the silence?

The destructive behaviors that emerge aren't random acts of self-sabotage; they are the predictable, desperate attempts of a numb soul trying to feel again.

In the next chapter, we will explore the terrifying consequences of this stage. Because the man who feels nothing will eventually do anything to feel something.

And that is where the real disaster begins.

CHAPTER 6
WHY THIS IS MORE DANGEROUS THAN BURNOUT

*"It is no measure of health to be well adjusted
to a profoundly sick society."*
Jiddu Krishnamurti

Rebecca stared at the screen on her phone; it was 3:47 a.m. when the message arrived from her husband's assistant: Mr. Thompson has been arrested for embezzling client funds. The partners are meeting at 8 a.m. to discuss damage control.

Twenty-four hours earlier, Thomas had been the most reliable partner at his firm. An impeccable reputation, a spotless record, and trusted with the largest accounts. The idea that he would steal money seemed impossible—not just because of his character, but because he had no apparent motive. His income was substantial, his lifestyle comfortable, and his financial situation stable.

But that's exactly what made his nulling out so dangerous. Thomas hadn't stolen the money because he needed it. He'd stolen it because transferring funds, covering his tracks, and managing the complex deception was the first thing in years that had generated any authentic emotional response. The risk, the secrecy, the skill required—it all made him feel more alive than any legitimate achievement had in years.

The partners, clients, and colleagues trying to understand Thomas's behavior kept looking for rational explanations: financial pressure, gambling debts, family crisis, substance abuse. They found none of these. What they did find was something far more disturbing—a highly competent professional who had systematically destroyed his career for no apparent reason other than the fact that destruction felt more real than success.

The danger with nulling out lies in its invisibility.

Burnout announces itself with exhaustion, and depression arrives with a heavy, visible sadness. But a person who is nulling out often appears to be thriving right up until the moment their life detonates.

Thomas's performance in the year leading up to his arrest had never been better. His composure was flawless, his reputation was spotless, and there were no missed deadlines, no struggles, or other warning signs that could have prompted a colleague or a loved one to intervene.

This is the unique and terrifying nature of high-functioning emptiness: **the internal braking system disappears.**

A person struggling with burnout is forced by fatigue to rest, and someone in the grip of anxiety is often constrained by caution, but Thomas had optimized away his own warning lights. He no longer felt the healthy hesitation that would make him think twice, nor the genuine attachment to his career that would make him protective of what he'd built. He could embezzle client funds with the same cold, emotional detachment he brought to any legitimate financial transaction. The moral gravity of his actions simply didn't register, because gravity requires an emotional weight he no longer possessed.

This lack of an internal brake often leads to an unconscious escalation. The behavior starts small—a minor rule bent, a slight ethical compromise that adds a flicker of excitement to an otherwise mechanical day. But because the natural stopping mechanisms have atrophied, the risks must get bigger and bigger to generate the same jolt. The search for any authentic feeling quickly becomes a desperate, reckless climb.

Perhaps most dangerously, a nulled-out state severs the connection to empathy. A nulled-out person can intellectually understand that their actions will harm others, but they cannot feel the weight of that harm. This isn't sociopathy; the capacity for empathy isn't gone forever. It has simply been optimized offline, along with every other authentic emotion.

The practical effect, however, is the same. It allows a good man like Thomas to make a decision that causes devastating harm, without the internal resistance that would have once made such a choice unthinkable.

Understanding the story of a man like Thomas is essential to understanding that the destructive behaviors that emerge from a nulled-out state are not random acts of self-sabotage. They are the predictable, desperate consequences of a soul that has been starved of feeling for too long.

In the next section, we will leave the diagnosis of the problem behind and begin the journey toward the solution. We will explore the practical, methodical, and deeply rewarding work of reconnection.

Because the path that led you away from yourself is also the path that can lead you back.

PART III
THE
CONSEQUENCES

*"The man who feels nothing will eventually do
anything to feel something."*

CHAPTER 7
WHEN FEELING NOTHING LEADS TO DOING ANYTHING

"The cave you fear to enter holds the treasure you seek."

Joseph Campbell

Margo checked her office phone for the tenth time. Nothing. It was their fifteenth anniversary, and for the first time, there were no flowers. A small knot of worry tightened in her stomach. Did he forget?

Then, her cell phone buzzed. It was Lance. The knot in her stomach instantly dissolved into a wave of giddy relief. Of course he hadn't forgotten. This was Lance—reliable, responsible Lance. This was just part of the surprise. She smiled, sure he was about to reveal a secret dinner reservation.

She opened the message: *I need to tell you something. I've been having an affair.*

The words blurred. The giddiness curdled into a cold shock that stole the air from her lungs. This? From the man who paid every bill on time, who attended every school function, who had just been promoted for his steady, unshakeable composure? It made no sense.

What Margo couldn't understand was that the affair had nothing to do with the other woman. It had nothing to do with problems in their marriage or dissatisfaction with their life together. The affair was Lance's desperate attempt to feel something—anything—after two years of feeling absolutely nothing.

For twenty-four months, Lance had been living in a state of complete emotional numbness while maintaining perfect external function. He excelled at work, provided for his family, and fulfilled every obligation without experiencing any genuine satisfaction, excitement, or even mild interest in his life.

The affair wasn't about sex, or romance, or escape. It was about the only situation that generated authentic emotional responses: the secrecy, the risk, the complexity of managing deception, the adrenaline of nearly being caught. For the first time in years, Lance felt genuinely alive—not because of the relationship itself, but because of the intensity required to maintain it.

When his conscience finally forced him to confess, he couldn't explain to Margo why he'd risked everything they'd built together for someone he didn't even love. Because the real answer—that destroying their marriage was the first thing that had made him feel real emotions in years—was too devastating for either of them to process.

This is what happens when feeling nothing becomes unbearable: people do anything to feel something, even if that something destroys everything they've worked to create.

The human psyche cannot sustain complete emotional emptiness indefinitely. When a man has been nulled-out for long enough, the internal pressure to experience a genuine feeling—any feeling—becomes an overwhelming, subconscious drive.

Lance didn't wake up one morning and decide to have an affair. It was a gradual descent, an unconscious drift toward any situation that could generate a spark in the void. It just so happened that the affair was the first opportunity that presented itself.

It began with small, seemingly harmless transgressions. Taking a slightly longer lunch break than allowed. Bending the expense account rules for a minor personal purchase. These weren't acts of greed; his salary was more than adequate. They were experiments in feeling. The slight transgression, the risk of getting caught, generated a faint jolt of something—guilt, excitement—that his perfectly optimized work life no longer could.

But the jolt from these small acts began to fade, so he found himself unconsciously testing boundaries in his relationships. A harmless flirtation with a colleague, a conversation that skirted the edge of appropriateness. This wasn't driven by a failing marriage, but by the simple fact that navigating social complexity required a level of authentic, in-the-moment engagement that his normal, scripted interactions had lost.

When even that lost its charge, the behavior escalated to something with real risk. A private, extended conversation with a colleague, meeting for drinks after work, sharing an emotional intimacy that he knew crossed a clear marital boundary. Each step was a gamble, and the gamble itself—the guilt, the fear of discovery, the thrill of the deception—was the prize. It was the only thing that made him feel.

The physical affair was the final, desperate act in this search for sensation. For months, Lance felt more alive maintaining the intricate machinery of his double life than he had felt in years. The constant risk, the emotional complexity, the anxiety, the passion—it was a full-spectrum emotional experience that stood in stark contrast to his flatlined, nulled-out existence. It was the detonation required to feel alive again.

CHAPTER 8
THE RIPPLE EFFECT: HOW NULLING OUT DESTROYS EVERYTHING AROUND YOU

"We are what we repeatedly do. Excellence, then,
is not an act, but a habit."

Aristotle

The email subject read Organizational Culture Assessment Results. Sam opened it, expecting the usual mix of engagement scores, satisfaction ratings, and improvement recommendations that consulting firms typically delivered.

Instead, he found a devastating analysis of what his leadership had unknowingly created.

"While productivity metrics and performance indicators suggest a highly successful organization," the report began, "employee interviews reveal a workplace culture characterized by emotional disconnection, strategic thinking divorced from genuine purpose, and widespread anxiety about authentic expression of concerns or creative ideas."

Sam read further, recognizing with growing horror the environment he'd built during his three years as CEO. High performance without engagement, execution without innovation, impressive efficiency alongside a complete absence of the passionate investment that had originally made the company successful.

He'd optimized his organization exactly the way he'd optimized himself—removing the messiness of authentic human response in favor of predictable, measurable outcomes. And just like his own internal transformation, it had worked perfectly by every external metric while destroying everything that actually mattered.

Sam was discovering what happens when nulled-out individuals reach positions of influence: they unconsciously create systems that produce more nulled-out individuals, spreading the disconnection until entire organizations lose the capacity for authentic human response.

Sam stared at the report, the consultant's words echoing in his head. This wasn't a case of a few disgruntled employees; he had built a system and a culture that systematically produced this disconnection.

He had never intended to create a toxic environment. He genuinely believed he was building an excellent organization by rewarding the very traits that had made him so successful. He promoted the people who showed perfect emotional control under pressure, who could think strategically without letting messy ethical concerns get in the way, and who executed his directives with machine-like efficiency. He had, in effect, created an advancement pipeline that filtered for nulled out traits and screened against authentic engagement.

The result was a leadership team of highly competent clones who could execute any strategy brilliantly, all while feeling no genuine investment in whether that strategy served a meaningful purpose.

He could see the consequences everywhere. The company, once a hub of innovation, now only excelled at optimizing existing processes. They could improve a workflow with mathematical precision, but they could no longer generate truly original ideas. When the market shifted, they were left behind, unable to respond creatively because true innovation requires a passionate, emotional investment in a problem—an investment his culture had systematically deemed "unprofessional."

More dangerously, he saw the ethical erosion. When a subordinate raised concerns about a new marketing campaign that was technically legal but morally questionable, the leadership team's response was chillingly academic. They evaluated it purely as a risk-management problem, calculating potential legal exposure and PR damage. What was completely absent from the room was a simple, gut-level moral revulsion. They had lost the ability to feel that a choice was simply wrong, regardless of its measurable risks.

Sam closed the email. He hadn't just built a successful company; he had built a perfect, efficient, and profitable machine for extinguishing the human soul, and he was its first and greatest success story.

He could now see the insidious logic of how the disconnection had spread. He had created an environment that achieved an impossible paradox: sky-high performance metrics alongside plummeting employee engagement. The company was a finely tuned engine running on an empty tank.

He remembered Jessica, a sharp marketing manager who used to light up their brainstorming sessions with creative, passionate ideas. He recalled how, under his leadership, he had "politely redirected" her and others like her to focus on conversion rates and cost efficiency, quietly teaching them that genuine excitement was less valuable than cold analysis. He had systematically trained his best people to suppress the very spark that had once made them brilliant.

It spread like a virus, an infection that bizarrely made its hosts more efficient. Tom, a senior developer, admitted he no longer cared if their products actually helped people; he just focused on code efficiency and delivery timelines. He even found himself internally scoffing at new hires who showed genuine excitement about the company's mission, seeing their passion as a form of naivete.

Tom had become a carrier. He was now unconsciously training the next generation to optimize themselves in the same way, creating a self-perpetuating cycle. The promotion system Sam had built naturally favored these newly optimized employees, creating a leadership pipeline that amplified the disconnection.

He looked at the names on his leadership team and realized with chilling certainty that not a single one of them could likely remember why they had originally joined the company, what they had hoped to build, or what would constitute meaningful success beyond hitting the next quarterly target. The contagion was complete.

Sam's story is a cautionary tale, not just for an individual, but for an entire way of thinking about success. It is the final, devastating consequence of a life and an organization built on a foundation of disconnection.

But this is not where the story has to end.

Having now explored the diagnosis, the descent, and the devastating consequences of nulling out, we can finally turn our attention to the most important part of this journey: the path back. Because if the path away from the self can be mapped, it can also be retraced.

In the final section of this book, we will leave the darkness of the diagnosis behind and step onto the solid ground of reconnection.

PART IV
THE
PATH BACK

"The path back is not a journey of becoming someone new. It is the brave, steady work of unbecoming everything that isn't you."

CHAPTER 9
OUT OF QUICKSAND, ONTO SOLID GROUND

"Your task is not to seek for love, but merely to seek and find all the barriers within yourself that you have built against it."

Rumi

Carol grew up in a household so authoritarian it bordered on tyranny. There were invisible rules everywhere—unspoken expectations that kept everyone walking on eggshells, and everyone was always planning for the day they could escape.

As a young child, Carol often thought about running away, hobo sack in tow. So profound was her aloneness and pain that she ached inside. She found solace perched high up in her father's tree, where she could privately sob while taking in the clouds as they moved gracefully across the sky. The beauty captivated her. The gentle breeze caressed her and gave her a fleeting moment of peace.

"It's just you and me, God."

She knew she had to get down before being caught in that tree. As she got older, she still loved climbing trees but retreated into scouting, academic excellence, music, and art—anything that provided a sanctuary from the tension in the home became her escape.

Carol was the middle child, the only girl among four siblings. She naturally gravitated toward the role of peacemaker. She learned this early when there was no option of winning, and she desperately wanted to prevent the whippings or surprise smacks her father would dish out from time to time. She learned to hide, remain still, and hold her breath while doing so. The closet became her favorite hiding place—back behind the suitcase, buried under as many clothes as she could pile up.

But Carol wasn't always unhappy. She loved school because it meant she wasn't home. Her school was all about building leaders, and her father basked in the spotlight of having children who shone academically. It was a win-win situation—a way for Carol to spend as little time as possible at home and grow her many interests. She had always wished "father dearest" would send her away to boarding school like one of his friends did with their children, but no—that would deprive him of the pleasure of tormenting his servant children.

When his fourth wife went by the wayside, Carol inherited full household duties at the age of eleven—cooking, cleaning, ironing, laundry, grocery shopping. She had always been responsible and worked hard, but now she was essentially running a household and taking care of five males while still a child.

Despite the obstacles, Carol managed to get into her first-choice private college—though only after her father forbade her from seeking admission to Ivy League schools. College was a wonderful fit, and she was finally able to step into who she felt she was—no pretense, no sugar-coating, no eggshells. Yet even then, her father tried to control her and interfere with her plans for medical school.

Medical school was a joyous revelation. Moving halfway across the country was a culture shock, but the people were wonderful. Carol was fully able to be who she envisioned herself to be—confident, authentic, self-possessed. But unbeknownst to her, this attracted attention, and the wrong type of attention.

To dissuade various suitors, she got involved with a classmate. However, this classmate figured out that she did not like public spectacle or the embarrassment such scenes caused. When he tried to create these situations, she would succumb to his wishes to avoid the humiliation. Carol finally became tired of being used and attempted to end whatever this warped relationship had become. Stepping up worked for a while, until one day, when he showed up at her door and laid it on thick. Against her better judgment, she invited him in. That was the wrong move.

The scene started light and playful, then became sensual. But when her back was turned, it turned into an assault. When it was over, she could barely move. The pain was excruciating. In that instance, she felt a murderous rage and knew if she could have moved, she might be serving life behind bars. She eventually made it to the bathroom, locked the door, and prayed for him to leave.

After a few days, Carol delivered a note to his mailbox – a threat and a promise. She did not call the authorities – that would have been messy. No, no, she decided to put distance between them, going half-time in medical school, and then taking a year off due to financial pressures and the need to distance herself from her classmates. So, for the next year, she volunteered with a youth group and worked in a plastics factory.

When Carol was called by the Chancellor to return to school, an evil empire had supplanted the humans who had been there when she left. The next two years were full of ongoing trials—threats, harassment, and bullying from the attending physicians who supervised her rotations. She later found out from her mentor that he was aware of this targeting—it wasn't paranoia; it was deliberate and organized institutional harassment.

But amidst the chaos, there were moments of profound joy and awe. The long nights spent sitting with dying cancer patients were not a burden; they were a refuge, an honor. Those quiet hours were the place where she felt a human connection. It was in those moments, paradoxically, that she felt most alive. But this genuine caring— or perhaps because of this genuine caring—made the Attendings despise her even more.

Carol started her residency after being promised that she wouldn't have to train where those hostile doctors were, and her mentor made good on that promise. Her time in Internal Medicine at a different medical school was a highlight of her first-year residency. But when the schools combined residency programs, the program fractured. Some attending psychiatrists, mired in institutional politics, simply stopped showing up to teach didactic sessions.

So, Carol decided to give them some time to get their act together and sought a program to solidify her skills in ambulatory medicine, a program that would only make her a stronger psychiatrist. Plus, she really needed a change of scenery.

Carol headed West. A program near the Bay Area had openings and beautiful scenery to boot. It felt like a reprieve. A place to finally breathe.

It wasn't.

This is where the training began to gobble up more and more of her life. Early after that assault, she had looked in the mirror and stated that there was something about her that attracted these predatory types, and she needed to destroy it to protect herself. She didn't consciously set out to destroy or split off a part of herself—but her training in Reno did that all by itself.

The internal medicine residency was intense and demanding. The days were long, but her patients were engaging. There were many days when she was up all night taking admissions and writing them up by hand—no computers back then—then needing to put together a presentation for the 8 AM pimp session where she'd be grilled extensively. No sleep. She had to gather X-rays, lab results, and know the underlying diagnoses and differentials, as well as round on all the patients before that meeting. By the time she left that program, she was working just shy of 110 hours per week.

The program had brought in a couple of first-year residents who were, frankly, disasters; disasters she was tasked to supervise. They wouldn't do their work, partied with the Attendings, and didn't take their role in caring for patients' lives seriously. One in particular would disappear for weeks at a time. Guess who had to cover his on-call duties? Is that a rhetorical question? Carol couldn't stand the thought of any patient under her care dangling on a precipice, but was told to keep her hands off "their" patients and only intervene if their patients were crashing. This created an enormous amount of stress. She didn't live her life that way.

When the program reneged on the initial plan towards double-boarding in psychiatry and internal medicine, and planned to put her in an ICU setting for two months straight—essentially 26 hours on, 22 hours off, Carol was furious. "That isn't ambulatory care." She would have to put up with nurses who would state "that isn't in my job description" and wouldn't alert her that a patient was crashing until after they'd crashed—she'd had enough.

After 18 months of slaving, Carol wanted to leave the program. But they didn't want to hear it. They had a manpower shortage, and she was to accept the decision. At that time, the contracts were for 6 months, not a year, and you were paid in arrears. So, they held her paycheck hostage, refusing to relinquish it, until she signed a new contract. However, before she signed, she requested that a thirty-day clause be added. So, after she signed it, with her check in hand, she said, "My thirty days start now."

During this time, instead of wearing regular clothes, Carol almost always wore surgical scrubs and a lab coat with her name embroidered on it. Her first name became "Doctor" and her last name became "Jack"—and that has stuck even to this day.

Afterward, she called her old mentor at her psychiatry residency, asking about coming back. His response was immediate: "Are you done proving what you set out to prove?" She didn't really know what that meant, but she said, "Yes." His response: "When can I expect you?"

When Carol returned to psychiatry, she was initially placed with a private psychiatrist to shadow him. She was extremely bored by that—really, profoundly bored. So, when her mentor asked if anyone wanted to spend a semester at the State Hospital, she jumped at the chance. It offered loads of autonomy and tons of interesting cases. She could use both her medical and psychiatric background, and she immediately started working with patients using an integrated approach.

When this rotation was completed, she sat for her licensing exam and passed without studying for it. Her outpatient clinical years were starting, where she would maintain a consistent patient load, keeping the same patients for the duration of her residency. It was at the beginning of this phase that her supervisors suggested that, to be a good psychiatrist, one should go through one's own therapy. Her question was always, "What was wrong with my approach to therapy?" As fate would have it, she found a most perfect match with a remarkable therapist who had a wealth of varied life experiences.

This therapist was the one who noticed that Carol had split off something unique to her persona. She started Carol on the road to reintegration. So yes, there were still crazy long hours running from ER to ER to Crisis Centers, but the person was coming back. Those activities that were uniquely Carol—the writing, the music, the songwriting, the connection to nature—were all being reintegrated.

Carol's life journey became a tapestry—rich and full, exquisitely varied in color. What she endured shaped who she would eventually become. She was better able to interpret the signals she was receiving and filter them through intuition and experience, thus being able to better help her clients as well as know when it was time for her to move on.

Carol knew early that she was never the type of person who could work in one setting for forty years. She shunned medical directorships and academia as those positions felt like traps and stagnation. She craved intensity and adventure, and yearned to deeply connect with people. Carol began to live life again. She continued to grow and continued to contribute, with no plan to retire, ever, grateful that this was her destiny.

CAROL IS ME.

The child hiding in the closet, the medical student who refused to be intimidated, the resident whose life was gobbled up by 110-hour weeks, the person who looked in the mirror and saw a stranger—all of it is my story. The difference is that the parts of myself that were once split off and hidden are now integrated to create a person who is both highly competent and genuinely alive.

This is why I understand nulling out from the inside out. I have lived every phase: the childhood conditioning that taught me to perform, the trauma that accelerated the disconnection, the brutal professional optimization that completed the erasure, and the slow, guided reintegration that brought me back to wholeness.

The quicksand nearly consumed me. But finding solid ground wasn't just my personal salvation; it became the foundation of my life's work. It is the reason I can now help others make the same journey.

Recovery from a nulled-out state is not about finding a perfect, mythical balance. It is about the real and often messy work of authentic integration. You do not have to choose between your success and your soul. The most sustainable success, the most fulfilling life, emerges from bringing your whole self to the challenges that matter.

The path back is real. And it is possible.

Now that we understand why these well-intentioned fixes so often fail, we can turn our attention to the real work. The path back is not one of rest, but of active, intentional, and sometimes awkward reconnection. It is a practical path, and it is the subject of our next chapter.

CHAPTER 10
THE PRACTICAL PATH TO RECOVERY

*"The journey of a thousand miles
begins with one step."*
Lao Tzu

When Sam finally admitted to himself that he was nulled-out, his first thought was a simple one: Blow it all up.

Quit the job. End the relationship. Move somewhere new. Anything to shock himself back to life. It was the high-achiever's instinct: Identify a problem and solve it with a single, dramatic, and decisive action.

But he quickly learned that a life is not a problem to be solved. Getting back from a nulled-out state is more like renovating a house while you're still living in it. You don't demolish the whole structure. You keep the parts that are strong, and you slowly, patiently, and sometimes messily, rebuild the rest.

THE INSPECTION: SEEING WHAT'S REAL

The first step in any renovation is an honest assessment. Sam had to first recognize the problem then stop pretending everything was fine. For one week, he simply paid attention, not to judge himself, but to see the truth. When did his reactions feel real? When did they feel scripted? When did he make a choice because he wanted something, versus because it was the most optimal or strategic move?

These are not easy observations. Sam had to be completely honest with everything he touched in that week. And to do that, he had to slow down.

He was tempted to treat this like another project to be perfected, with detailed schedules for "authenticity practices" and spreadsheets to track his progress. But that was the old way of thinking. He had to accept that this work would be messy, inconsistent, and gradual.

During his inspection, he found something crucial. Even in a house that seemed abandoned, a few lights were still on. He discovered he still had genuine, unfaked preferences about food. Certain music still stirred something in him. Some work projects still felt like they actually mattered. These small pockets of life didn't need to be rebuilt. They were proof that the person he used to be was still in there, just buried under years of optimization.

THE FIRST SMALL FIXES: LEARNING TO USE NEW TOOLS

The renovation didn't begin with a sledgehammer. It began with a series of tiny, almost imperceptible choices. He started with a coffee shop, choosing one based on its appeal, not on its convenience. He took a different route home from work, following a road that looked interesting, not the one that was fastest.

Each small choice was an act of practice. He was trying to hear a signal that was so faint it was almost a whisper. At first, it felt strange, even irresponsible. A part of him, conditioned by years of treating optimization as a virtue, screamed in protest. The guilt about being "inefficient" was real. Choosing a restaurant because the food sounded appealing instead of convenient and healthy felt like a reckless indulgence.

But each "inefficient" choice proved something vital: he could follow these faint, internal signals, and the world would not fall apart. He started digging up old parts of himself, listening to music from college, visiting places that once felt meaningful. Most felt flat at first. But some sparked a faint echo of the person who used to live there, and those echoes gave him a direction to follow.

Perhaps the hardest part was relearning curiosity for its own sake. He forced himself to read about things that interested him with no professional angle, to ask questions that served no strategic purpose. His internal optimizer hated this. It generated anxiety about "wasted time." But he was discovering that curiosity without an agenda is the soil in which a real life grows.

THE MAJOR REMODEL: INTEGRATING WORK AND LIFE

As the whispers of his own preferences grew stronger, the real challenge began. He had to figure out how to be this emerging person in a world that had been built for the old, optimized version of him.

This was most difficult in his marriage. His wife had learned to relate to a man who efficiently handled his responsibilities and had no real opinions on personal matters. When he started having genuine preferences about vacation spots, weekend plans, or family decisions, it created tension. Their entire system had been built around the silence of his desires. Now he had them, and they had to renegotiate everything.

Instead of ending relationships, he began to gradually introduce more of his real self. He started expressing his own opinions instead of strategically appropriate ones. He suggested activities he actually wanted to do. Some friendships, the ones based purely on networking, faded naturally. Others, the real ones, got deeper. Both were okay.

At work, he faced his biggest fear: that reconnecting with himself would make him less effective. That caring would make him less objective. The opposite proved true. His authentic investment in problems made his strategic thinking more creative. His values provided a clearer filter for making tough decisions. His emotional engagement generated a sustainable motivation that the adrenaline of pure optimization never could. He discovered that people will follow a leader who is competently human far more readily than one who is just a competent machine.

LIVING IN THE NEW HOUSE: MAINTENANCE AND PREVENTION

The renovation is never truly "done." Reconnection, like physical fitness, requires ongoing practice to prevent sliding back into the old patterns.

Sam developed daily "check-ins," brief moments to ask himself: "How do I actually feel about this meeting?" "What do I genuinely want for lunch?" These weren't major decisions. They were simply daily practice in accessing his own internal signals.

He also got better at recognizing the early warning signs of a regression. When his decisions started to feel purely efficiency-based, when conversations felt scripted, when his achievements started to feel hollow again—these became his alarms. They were signals to refocus on his practices before he drifted too far.

He learned that this work required a supportive environment. He began to intentionally seek out professional contexts where passionate investment was valued, and relationships where genuine engagement mattered more than a flawless performance. He was creating a life where staying human felt natural, not like a constant, exhausting effort.

Recovery from a nulled-out state is not a destination. It is the ongoing, courageous practice of choosing integration over optimization, of honoring who you are, what you've built, and the core principles by which you want to live.

CHAPTER 11
STAYING CONNECTED:
PREVENTION AND MAINTENANCE

"Yesterday I was clever, so I wanted to change the world. Today I am wise, so I am changing myself."

Rumi

Three years after Michael began to reconnect with his own life, he faced a new challenge that tested his resolve. His company was taken over by corporate sharks—the kind of place where they measure your worth by how efficiently you can and are willing to crush your own soul. It was the same type of environment that had turned him into a walking corpse the first time.

New bosses rolled in with their spreadsheets and their metrics. The message was clear: be a robot or get out. They wanted people who could make decisions without pesky things like conscience getting in the way.

Michael's coworkers started caving immediately. Who could blame them? It was easier to shut off your humanity than explain to your mortgage company that you got fired for having feelings.

But Michael had learned something in those three years. He had learned how to stay human in places designed to kill that very thing.

PART I: THE DAILY PRACTICE OF STAYING ALIVE

Getting your life back isn't a one-time fix. It is an ongoing practice, more like staying sober than setting a broken bone. It is a daily choice, a daily effort. The world will constantly offer you reasons to go back to sleep.

Staying connected requires vigilance. If you stop paying attention for too long, the erosion begins. It doesn't happen overnight. It's a series of little compromises, until one day you look in the mirror and don't recognize the person staring back.

Michael learned to watch for the whispers that he was drifting back toward the void: decisions feeling automatic instead of chosen; wins at work feeling empty; conversations turning into scripts.

To counter this, he built a simple, daily architecture of self-connection:

- **The Morning Check-In:** He started every day with a simple question: "What do I actually want from today?" Not "What do I need to accomplish?" but what did he, as a person, want from the next sixteen hours? Five minutes. That's all it took to set the course for his day.

- **The Midday Gut Check:** Before any important decision, he would pause and ask: "Am I choosing this because it makes sense, or because a part of me truly wants it?" He'd spent years only asking the first question. Adding the second one back in changed everything.

- **The Evening Inventory:** At the end of each day, he'd take a mental inventory: When had he felt alive? When had he been sleepwalking? Not to judge, but simply to notice the patterns, steering himself toward more of the life-giving and away from the soul-crushing.

PART II: THE ART OF THE TRANSLATION

When the corporate vultures took over, Michael didn't fight them head-on. That would have been career suicide. Instead, he learned to speak their language while protecting his own. He learned the art of translation.

In meetings obsessed with cost-cutting, he'd ask: "How do we hit these numbers without destroying the very thing that makes us good at our jobs?"

In strategy sessions focused on pure efficiency, he'd say: "What's the approach that gets us the best long-term results, not just the fastest short-term wins?"

He was advocating for human considerations using the business language they could understand. He also found the others—the people who still cared about doing good work, not just efficient work. They didn't form a resistance. They just quietly supported each other in bringing their whole selves to the office.

PART III: EMERGENCY PROTOCOLS FOR A NUMB STATE

Even with his practices, there were brutal periods when Michael felt himself slipping back into machine mode. When he caught himself making decisions like a computer, feeling nothing, treating people like obstacles—he had a protocol in place that would act as his compass.

1. **Acknowledge:** First, he had to admit it was happening, instead of pretending everything was fine.

2. **Diagnose:** He'd figure out what had overwhelmed his defenses. A crazy deadline? Relationship stress? A workload that left no room for being human?

3. **Intensify:** He would then double down on the practices that brought him back to life—more check-ins, more choices based on what felt right, more time with people who reminded him he was a person, not just a job title.

PART IV: BUILDING A LIFE THAT PROTECTS YOU

Ultimately, Michael realized that just surviving in soul-crushing environments wasn't enough. The real work was to redesign his entire existence around a single principle: creating the conditions where staying human felt natural, not like a constant effort.

This meant career moves that aligned with his values, not just his ambitions. It meant relationships that encouraged real expression, not just appropriate behavior. He wasn't trying to escape the world. He was building a life that actively supported his own humanity.

He wasn't preaching or trying to convert anyone. He was just living proof that you don't have to choose between being successful and be-ing human. The people who were ready for that message saw it. And for the ones who weren't, his life was a quiet, standing invitation.

The real solution to this epidemic isn't just about helping individuals reconnect. It's about creating cultures where that disconnection never happens in the first place. Michael's story isn't just about one man getting his life back. It's about what becomes possible when we stop treating our humanity and our success as enemies.

CHAPTER 12
THE INTEGRATED LIFE:
SUCCESS THAT SUSTAINS

"The privilege of a lifetime is to become who you truly are."

Carl Jung

Michael discovered that the most profound change wasn't in his bank account or his title, but in the end of the exhausting internal war he had been fighting.

For years, the price of his performance had been the suppression of his own true self. His life was a constant, draining negotiation between the role he had to play and the person he was. The work of in-tegration wasn't about finding a better balance between these two competing forces; it was about fusing them into a unified whole. It was the discovery that his most effective work could emerge from his deepest, most genuine engagement.

The first thing he noticed was the energy. When your strategic thinking serves your own principles, work is no longer a grind; it's a current that carries you. This wasn't the temporary adrenaline of closing a deal, but the deep, sustainable energy that comes from operating as a whole person.

Perhaps most surprisingly, his creativity exploded. When he allowed his sharp, strategic mind to be informed by his passionate investment in the outcome, he began to see possibilities that cold analysis could never access. Breakthrough solutions became the natural result of a mind that was no longer at war with its own heart.

His achievements finally felt satisfying. His relationships deepened. He could finally bring his whole self to the table, not just his optimized performance. He was no longer a ghost haunting a successful life; he was finally inhabiting it.

This transformation, however, was not confined to his internal world. His newfound integration became his greatest professional asset. He began to lead with "passionate competence," fusing his sharp, strategic mind with a real investment in the outcomes. Instead of presenting a fortress of data, he now presented a compelling vision that served both profit and principle. His colleagues and clients no longer just respected his analysis; they felt a connection to his purpose. This was the source of his new, more powerful influence.

The real legacy of an integrated leader, however, isn't in a single victory; it's in the culture they build and the people they inspire.

Michael's leadership began to change everything around him. His team meetings, once sterile data reviews, now included honest and open discussions about the "why" behind the "what." He started hiring for values alignment alongside technical skill and promoting people based on their capacity for true leadership.

This wasn't inefficient sentiment. It was sophisticated leadership. He recognized that genuine engagement was the essential fuel for sustainable high performance, not a luxury that competed with it. His teams appreciated recognition of their abilities and input, and began to generate more novel approaches and sustained excellence, because they were finally operating from a place of both competence and deep personal investment.

The change even followed him home, becoming the most important legacy he would ever create. His teenage children grew up observing a father who brought both strategic genius and real passion to his work. They learned, through his daily example, that success did not require self-erasure. They learned to make choices that honored both their responsibilities and their interests, because that's what a fulfilled life looks like.

This is more than just good parenting. It is the interruption of a dangerous inheritance. He was teaching his children an emotional fluency that would make them immune to the very condition he had to recover from. He was giving them the one thing his own upbringing never could: a living blueprint for an integrated life. They would never have to "reconnect" later, because he was teaching them never to disconnect in the first place.

Michael's journey from a nulled-out executive to an integrated leader shows what becomes possible when we stop treating our inner truth and our success as competing priorities. His story isn't about becoming a perfect man; it's the story of a capable man who finally gave himself permission to become a whole one.

The integrated life is not a destination. It is a way of living you choose—daily, consciously, courageously. The question isn't whether integration is possible—Michael's story proves that it is. The real question is whether you are ready to stop choosing between a life that looks good on paper and one that feels good in your soul, and start discovering the profound power that is unleashed when you finally pursue both.

CONCLUSION
FROM NULLED-OUT TO FULLY ALIVE

Michael received an email from a young man who had heard him speak about his experience with 'nulling out,' and smiled to himself, knowing he had helped someone identify it in their own life.

"I heard you speak at a leadership conference," he said. "You were the first person to put a name to something I've been feeling for years. I don't know how to change this without destroying my career. Can you help me understand where to start?"

Michael recognized the courage it takes to confront such feelings, and it echoed his own moment of terrifying clarity years earlier, when he admitted that the life he constructed felt like a cage. That email was a flare in the dark, a signal from someone else who was beginning the journey from emptiness to a fully present life.

The young man in that email was standing at the same crossroads I had faced.

And perhaps, as you finish this book, you are standing there right now.

You may have recognized the stories and patterns in your own life, giving a name to the silent ache you've carried for years. You know you are not broken, and you know you are not alone. You just don't know the path from point A to point B.

The journey you are contemplating is about rediscovering your authentic self, the person you were before societal pressures and expectations dictated your choices; the person you were meant to be. It is a process of reconnection, not replacement. You don't have to abandon the competence and drive that have made you successful; you only need to re-infuse them with the authentic, human core you may have been forced to suppress.

This is not a sudden, dramatic overhaul that will create chaos in your life. It is a gradual, patient, and courageous process. You will learn to treat your own authentic responses—your preferences, your values, your intuition—as valid and essential data. It is the art of discovering that you do not have to live in a world of false "either/or" choices between success and fulfillment.

The journey onward is about integration. It is about bringing your whole self back online. Reading this book was the first, essential step in recognizing and naming the feelings you've experienced. With this newfound understanding, you now hold the map to guide your journey.

But a map is not the journey.

The path to reconnection is a practice, a choice you make every day. So, the final, most important question is: Where do you go from here?

To support you as you begin this vital work, I have created two distinct pathways. Consider your current needs. Start with the "planner" and then assess whether you need more guidance.

PATHWAY 1:
—
THE RECONNECTION PLANNER

This workbook is available to all as a thank you for reading this book. It's a free download and my gift to you. This planner is designed to help you put the exercises from this book to immediate use.

Download your free planner at:

NullingOut.com/thepath

PATHWAY 2:

—

THE RECLAMATION DISCOVERY SESSION

When you have completed the self-diagnosis and work laid out in the planner, you may want personal assistance. You are invited to apply for a discovery session, which is a private, 1-on-1 working session to determine if there is a fit. It is an intensive process for men who are serious about doing the work and ready to invest in a rapid, guided transformation.

Due to the intensive nature of these sessions, I only accept a limited number of applicants per month.

To learn more and begin the application process, visit:

CherylJack.com/Apply

APPENDIX A:
THE NULLING OUT DIAGNOSTIC TOOLKIT

Here's a comprehensive self-assessment that could help readers identify their level of disconnection:

THE NULLING OUT ASSESSMENT SCALE

Instructions: Read each statement and rate how accurately it describes your current experience using this scale:

- 5 = Always true

- 4 = Often true

- 3 = Sometimes true

- 2 = Rarely true

- 1 = Never true

SECTION 1: ACHIEVEMENT AND SATISFACTION

1. When I reach professional milestones, I feel mainly relief that I didn't fail rather than genuine satisfaction

2. My accomplishments feel hollow even when others congratulate me

3. I can't remember the last time I felt genuinely excited about achieving something

4. Success feels mechanical—like checking boxes rather than meaningful progress

5. I find myself asking, "Is this all there is?" after major achievements

SECTION 2: DECISION-MAKING PATTERNS

6. I make most decisions based on what's most efficient rather than what appeals to me

7. When asked what I want (restaurant, movie, weekend activity), I genuinely don't know

8. I choose options that make logical sense even when they don't feel right

9. I evaluate opportunities primarily through strategic analysis rather than genuine interest

10. I struggle to remember what I actually enjoyed before I became "responsible"

SECTION 3: EMOTIONAL RESPONSIVENESS

11. I feel emotionally flat about experiences that should be meaningful

12. I go through conversations on autopilot, saying appropriate things without genuine engagement

13. I can analyze situations clearly but feel no emotional investment in the outcomes

14. I perform enthusiasm rather than feel it naturally

15. I've lost access to strong preferences about most things

SECTION 4: RELATIONSHIPS AND SOCIAL INTERACTIONS

16. My family members sometimes seem like strangers even though we live together

17. I maintain relationships through consistent behavior rather than authentic connection

18. I say what people want to hear rather than what I actually think

19. Social interactions feel like performances I need to execute well

20. I feel disconnected from others even when I'm being socially successful

SECTION 5: WORK AND PROFESSIONAL LIFE

21. I can excel at my job while feeling completely detached from the work

22. I make professional decisions without considering whether they align with my values

23. I've optimized my work performance while losing interest in the actual outcomes

24. I function like a sophisticated machine rather than an engaged professional

25. My work quality is high, but I feel no genuine investment in what I'm producing

SECTION 6: PHYSICAL AND BEHAVIORAL INDICATORS

26. I eat meals without tasting them or noticing what I actually want

27. I sleep adequately but never feel truly rested

28. I maintain self-care routines mechanically rather than as nurturing activities

29. I exercise efficiently but feel disconnected from my body

30. I follow optimal schedules rather than responding to what I actually need

SCORING GUIDE:

Add up your total score:

120-150 points: Severe Nulling Out You're operating almost entirely from optimization with very little access to authentic responses. Consider this a priority for immediate attention. The practices in Chapter 10 are essential starting points.

90-119 points: Moderate Nulling Out You maintain some connection to authentic responses but have optimized away significant portions of your capacity for genuine engagement. Focus on the reconnection practices in Chapters 9-10.

60-89 points: Early Stage Nulling Out You're showing warning signs but still have substantial access to authentic responses. The prevention strategies in Chapter 11 can help you avoid deeper disconnection.

30-59 points: Minimal Disconnection You maintain good connection to authentic responses with only occasional optimization override. Focus on maintaining this connection as pressures increase.

Below 30 points: Integrated Living You successfully balance strategic thinking with authentic engagement. You can serve as a model for others struggling with disconnection.

THE QUICK DAILY CHECK-IN

For ongoing self-monitoring, ask yourself these three questions each evening:

1. **Authenticity Check:** "When today did I feel most like myself versus most like I was performing a role?"

2. **Decision Quality:** "What decisions today were based on genuine preference versus pure optimization?"

3. **Energy Assessment:** "What activities today energized me versus drained me, and why?"

RED FLAG INDICATORS

Seek immediate support if you notice:

- Complete inability to access personal preferences about anything
- Making increasingly risky decisions just to feel something
- Professional success that feels entirely meaningless
- Relationships that feel purely transactional
- Persistent sense that you're watching your life happen to someone else

THE VALUES RECONNECTION EXERCISE

If your assessment indicates disconnection, try this:

1. List ten things you cared about before you became "successful"

2. Identify which of these you've optimized away

3. Choose one small way to reconnect with each lost value

4. Practice making one decision daily based on authentic preference rather than efficiency

This assessment isn't a clinical diagnostic tool but a framework for recognizing disconnection patterns and beginning the reconnection process described throughout the book.

APPENDIX B:
UNDERSTANDING THE ARCHITECTURE OF NULLING OUT

For readers who want to understand the psychological framework behind Carol's journey and how it applies to recovery from nulling out

My journey from that terrified child hiding behind suitcases to someone who can say "life is a delicious journey" illustrates every phase of how nulling out develops—and how recovery is possible.

THE FOUNDATION: EARLY CONDITIONING

The nulling out process began long before my medical career. In my father's household, I learned the fundamental lesson that would later make me vulnerable to complete optimization: genuine responses are dangerous.

The invisible rules, the eggshells, the need to become a peacekeeper—these taught me that my genuine reactions, needs, and preferences were not just unwelcome, they were actively threatening to my survival. I learned to suppress my responses and perform whatever version of myself kept me safest.

This is where nulling out begins for most high achievers: not in boardrooms, but in childhood environments where authenticity becomes a liability and performance becomes protection.

THE ACCELERATION: TRAUMA AND SYSTEMATIC TARGETING

The assault in medical school wasn't just personal trauma—it was the catalyst that accelerated my disconnection from true responses. When I looked in the mirror afterward and decided to "destroy" whatever attracted predatory behavior, I was identifying my confidence and self-possession as the problem.

This is a crucial distinction: I wasn't naturally weak or inclined toward people-pleasing. I was systematically broken down by someone who recognized my specific vulnerabilities around authority and public humiliation—vulnerabilities created by my childhood survival patterns.

The subsequent targeting by attending physicians wasn't paranoia; it was confirmed systematic harassment. But rather than fighting back with in-your-face outrage, I learned to optimize my way around these obstacles. Each challenge taught me to suppress more of my true and immediate responses in favor of strategic survival.

THE COMPLETION: PROFESSIONAL OPTIMIZATION

The internal medicine residency completed what trauma had started. Working 110 hours per week, covering for "the 'problem children' colleagues," being forced to watch patients approach dangerous precipices—this wasn't just demanding training, it was their attempt to interfere with my professional judgment.

Every day, I learned to silence my genuine concerns about patient care, to suppress my responses to unfair treatment. Every day there was an assault on my need for sleep and recovery that I had to just "man up" and take. I became extraordinarily competent while struggling against becoming disconnected from any investment in the outcomes, and it did reach a breaking point.

The transformation of "Carol" into "Doctor Jack" was the final phase—even my name disappeared behind professional identity. I had successfully optimized myself into a highly functional professional who felt little to nothing for my own life aside from anger.

THE RECOGNITION: WHEN COMPETENCE BECOMES PRISON

The boredom I felt when shadowing that private psychiatrist was actually a crucial sign. Someone who is nulled out can't be engaged by anything that doesn't require survival-level intensity. I had become so disconnected from responses that only extreme challenges (like the State Hospital) could penetrate that space.

My mentor's question—"Are you done proving what you set out to prove?"—was recognition that I had been trying to demonstrate I was bright enough, tough enough to survive anything. But, in retrospect, in proving I could endure any level of mistreatment, I had inadvertently trained myself to endure rather than exit -- even when situations were genuinely intolerable --because I knew they were temporary obstacles to attaining my goal.

THE RECOVERY: REINTEGRATION, NOT REPLACEMENT

The most important lesson from my recovery is that my true self wasn't destroyed by nulling out—it was suppressed and could be reintegrated. My therapist didn't try to "fix" anything wrong with me; she recognized that something essential had been split off and helped me bring it back online.

The writing, music, songwriting, and connection to nature weren't new interests I developed—they were core aspects of my being that I gradually reconnected with. My recovery wasn't about becoming someone different; it was about becoming whole again.

THE INTEGRATION: COMPETENCE PLUS AUTHENTICITY

What my story demonstrates is that you don't have to choose between professional competence and being true to yourself, to your version of your life. The expertise I developed during my nulled-out years didn't disappear when I reintegrated—it became more effective because I could integrate my voice, my insights into the whole, to improve outcomes. It was no longer about work and survival.

Today, I can maintain professional authority while trusting my responses. I can make strategic decisions that also honor my genuine values. I can be "Doctor Jack" when the situation requires that expertise while remaining fully present as me, my true self.

THE PURPOSE: FROM SURVIVAL TO SERVICE

Perhaps most importantly, my experience of complete nulling out and subsequent recovery is what allows me to recognize these patterns in others and guide them toward reintegration. I don't just understand this phenomenon theoretically—I lived it, survived it, and found the path back to wholeness.

Every phase of my journey—from childhood conditioning through professional optimization to authentic reintegration—shapes the framework I've developed for helping others navigate their own quicksand and find their own solid ground.

APPENDIX C:
THE RECONNECTION FIELD MANUAL

☐   A FIELD MANUAL FOR THE PATH BACK

☐   RESOURCES FOR PROFESSIONAL SUPPORT

☐   FINDING THE RIGHT TYPE OF PROFESSIONAL HELP

☐   WHEN TO SEEK PROFESSIONAL SUPPORT

CONSIDER PROFESSIONAL GUIDANCE IF YOU:

- Score above 90 on the Nulling Out Assessment
- Notice persistent inability to access your preferences
- Are engaging in increasingly risky behaviors to feel something
- Feel completely disconnected from all relationships
- Experience thoughts of self-harm or suicide
- Are unable to make progress with self-directed reconnection efforts after 3–6 months

TYPES OF PROFESSIONAL SUPPORT

1. SPECIALIZED COACHING (RECOMMENDED FIRST OPTION)

LOOK FOR COACHES WHO UNDERSTAND:

- The difference between nulling out and burnout/depression

- Integration approaches rather than traditional work-life balance
- High-achiever dynamics and optimization patterns
- Reconnection practices rather than just performance improvement

QUESTIONS TO ASK POTENTIAL COACHES:

- "How do you work with successful people who feel empty despite their achievements?"
- "What's your understanding of the difference between burnout and what this book calls nulling out?"
- "How do you help clients integrate authenticity with professional effectiveness?"
- "What's your approach when someone has lost access to their genuine preferences?"

RED FLAGS IN COACHING:

- Focuses only on goal-setting and performance optimization
- Dismisses authenticity concerns as "soft" or impractical
- Promises quick fixes or dramatic life changes
- Doesn't understand the unique challenges of high-achiever disconnection

2. THERAPEUTIC SUPPORT

Therapy can be helpful when combined with coaching, but seek therapists who:

- Understand that nulling out isn't depression or anxiety
- Focus on reconnection rather than just symptom management
- Have experience with high-functioning individuals

- Don't pathologize optimization skills while addressing disconnection

THERAPEUTIC APPROACHES THAT MAY HELP:

- **Acceptance and Commitment Therapy (ACT):** Focuses on values clarification and authentic living
- **Gestalt Therapy:** Emphasizes present-moment awareness and your humanistic response
- **Somatic Therapy:** Helps reconnect with body signals and physical responses
- **Existential Therapy:** Addresses meaning and purpose questions

THERAPEUTIC APPROACHES THAT OFTEN MISS THE MARK:

- **Pure Cognitive Behavioral Therapy (CBT):** May reinforce optimization patterns
- **Psychoanalytic approaches:** May over-focus on past trauma that didn't cause the nulling out
- **Traditional depression/anxiety treatments:** Address different conditions entirely

ORGANIZATIONAL SUPPORT RESOURCES

1. EXECUTIVE COACHING PROGRAMS

LOOK FOR PROGRAMS THAT ADDRESS:

- Sustainable leadership rather than just performance optimization
- Values-based decision-making alongside strategic thinking
- Employee engagement through true-to-self leadership
- Long-term effectiveness rather than short-term results

2. LEADERSHIP DEVELOPMENT WITH INTEGRATION FOCUS

RECOMMENDED ORGANIZATIONS AND PROGRAMS:

- Programs that explicitly address meaning and purpose in leadership
- Executive education that includes values clarification components
- Leadership retreats that focus on sustainable approaches rather than just efficiency
- Mentorship programs pairing participants with integrated leaders

CRISIS RESOURCES

IMMEDIATE MENTAL HEALTH SUPPORT IF EXPERIENCING THOUGHTS OF SELF-HARM:

- **National Suicide Prevention Lifeline:** 988
- **Crisis Text Line:** Text HOME to 741741
- **International Association for Suicide Prevention:**

  https://www.iasp.info/suicidalthoughts/

PROFESSIONAL BURNOUT RESOURCES

IF UNSURE WHETHER YOU'RE EXPERIENCING NULLING OUT VS. BURNOUT:

- Maslach Burnout Inventory (professional assessment)

  https://www.mindgarden.com/117-maslach-burnout-inventory-mbi

- Workplace mental health programs through Employee Assistance Programs (EAP)
- Occupational health specialists familiar with executive stress

SUPPORT COMMUNITIES AND GROUPS

1. PROFESSIONAL NETWORKS FOR INTEGRATED LIVING

LOOK FOR:

- Industry groups focused on meaningful work rather than just networking
- Professional associations with values-based leadership components
- Mastermind groups for purpose-driven professionals
- Alumni networks from values-focused business programs

2. ONLINE COMMUNITIES

HELPFUL ONLINE RESOURCES:

- Forums for high-achievers questioning traditional success metrics
- LinkedIn groups focused on meaningful leadership
- Professional development communities emphasizing integration
- Industry-specific groups discussing purpose alongside performance

WARNING SIGNS OF UNHELPFUL ONLINE COMMUNITIES:

- Focus on dramatic life changes rather than integration
- Anti-success or anti-achievement messaging
- Oversimplified solutions to complex problems
- Lack of understanding of high-achiever dynamics

SELF-DIRECTED LEARNING RESOURCES

BOOKS FOR DEEPER UNDERSTANDING

COMPLEMENTARY READING THAT SUPPORTS INTEGRATION:

- Drive by Daniel Pink (motivation and purpose)
- Flow by Mihaly Csikszentmihalyi (engagement and optimal experience)
- The Purpose-Driven Life by Rick Warren (meaning and values)
- Essentialism by Greg McKeown (strategic choices aligned with values)
- The Gifts of Imperfection by Brené Brown (authenticity and vulnerability)

ASSESSMENT TOOLS FOR ONGOING MONITORING

1. VALUES CLARIFICATION ASSESSMENTS:

- Values In Action (VIA) Character Strengths Survey

  https://www.viacharacter.org/

- Rokeach Value Survey (RVS)

  https://scales.arabpsychology.com/s/rokeach-value-survey-rvs/

- Personal Values Assessment from various coaching organizations

2. PROFESSIONAL SATISFACTION ASSESSMENTS:

- Job satisfaction surveys that include meaning components
- Employee engagement assessments
- Purpose-at-work evaluation tools

CREATING YOUR SUPPORT TEAM

THE INTEGRATED SUPPORT APPROACH

CONSIDER ASSEMBLING:

1. Primary coach or therapist who understands nulling out specifically
2. Professional mentor who models integrated success
3. Peer support group of others working on similar integration
4. Family/relationship support for personal life integration
5. Spiritual/philosophical guidance for meaning and purpose questions

QUESTIONS FOR EVALUATING ANY PROFESSIONAL SUPPORT

1. "Do they understand that I'm successful professionally but empty personally?"
2. "Can they help me integrate authenticity with continued high performance?"
3. "Do they focus on reconnection rather than just symptom management?"
4. "Are they familiar with high-achiever dynamics and optimization patterns?"

5. "Do they support gradual integration rather than dramatic life changes?"

COST AND INSURANCE CONSIDERATIONS

a. COACHING COSTS

- Executive coaching: $200-500+ per hour
- Group coaching programs: $2,000-10,000 for multi-month programs
- Online coaching programs: $500-3,000

b. THERAPY COSTS

- Individual therapy: $100-300 per session
- Many insurance plans cover therapy for depression/anxiety but may not cover "life satisfaction" concerns
- Employee Assistance Programs often provide 3–8 free sessions

c. INVESTMENT PERSPECTIVE

CONSIDER PROFESSIONAL SUPPORT AS AN INVESTMENT IN:

- Preventing destructive behaviors that could destroy career/relationships
- Increasing long-term effectiveness and satisfaction
- Avoiding costs of continued disconnection (health impacts, relationship damage, career plateau)

RED FLAGS: WHEN TO CHANGE PROVIDERS

SEEK DIFFERENT SUPPORT IF YOUR PROVIDER:

- Treats nulling out as standard depression or anxiety

- Focuses only on work-life balance without addressing integration

- Encourages dramatic life changes without gradual reconnection work

- Doesn't understand the unique challenges of high-achiever disconnection

- Makes you feel pathologized for your optimization skills

- Promises quick fixes or oversimplified solutions

Remember: The goal isn't to find someone who will fix you, but someone who can support your own reconnection process while honoring both your competencies and your need for honest and true engagement.

APPENDIX D:
A GUIDE FOR SPOUSES, PARTNERS, AND LEADERS

You may be reading this not because you see yourself in these pages, but because you see someone you love or lead. You sense a profound disconnect, that they are physically present but emotionally absent. They are meeting every obligation, yet their spark is gone. You feel a growing distance you can't name, and your concern is met with a calm, logical assurance that "everything is fine."

You are not imagining it. You are likely living with or leading a person who is nulled-out. This appendix is for you.

Because the support required from an intimate partner is fundamentally different from that of a professional leader, this guide is split into two sections. The first part is for spouses and partners. The second part is for leaders and managers. Shall we begin?

PART 1: FOR SPOUSES & PARTNERS

The Lived Experience: A Peculiar Form of Abandonment

The families of nulled-out individuals often describe a strange sense of loss. Margo, Lance's wife from Chapter 7, lived this reality for two years. Lance attended every family dinner. He participated in conversations and fulfilled every expectation of a husband and father. But Margo felt like she was married to a very competent stranger.

"He would ask how my day was and listened," she explained, "but I could tell the part of him that would genuinely care was turned off. It was like talking to a sophisticated customer service representative trained to simulate interest."

This creates a damaging form of gaslighting. Family members sense something is missing, but they can't point to any specific failure.

When Margo discovered Lance's affair, her shock wasn't just about the infidelity. "I realized I'd been living with someone who was essentially dead inside," she said. "That was almost harder to process than the betrayal itself."

How to Offer Support: A "Do This, Not That" Framework

Approaching a nulled-out partner requires a strategy of gentle reflection, not intervention.

- **DO: Focus on Shared Experience.** Use neutral observations about your shared life. "I was thinking about how we used to laugh planning our trips. I miss that feeling with you." This is an observation of a shared memory, not a critique of their current state.

  o **DON'T: Accuse or Diagnose.** Saying "You seem unhappy" or "I think you're nulled-out" will be met with a logical denial, because they don't feel unhappy.

- **DO: Speak From Your Own Feeling of Loss.** Center your experience of their disconnection using "I" statements. "Lately, I've been feeling lonely, even when we're in the same room," is a vulnerable truth, not an attack.

  o **DON'T: Make It Their Fault.** "You are being distant" puts them on the defensive.

- **DO: Create Low-Pressure Openings.** The goal is not a confrontation. It's an invitation. Try, "I'm going for a quiet walk, I'd love it if you'd join me." The shared silence on a walk can be more connecting than a forced conversation.

  o **DON'T: Ask Demanding Questions**. "Why are you like this?" is an impossible question. Even "What's wrong?" assumes they know, and they likely don't.

Your Role (and Its Limits)

It is crucial to understand that you cannot reconnect someone else. The journey back from a nulled-out state is a profoundly internal one.

Your role is not to be their therapist, but to be a safe harbor for when they decide they are ready to begin the work. Protecting your own well-being is not selfish; it is essential.

PART 2: FOR LEADERS & MANAGERS

As a leader, you are in a unique and challenging position. You sense the disengagement, but you must operate within professional boundaries. Your role is not to be a counselor, but an observant, resourceful, and supportive manager.

What to Look For: Observable, Professional Metrics

You cannot comment on an employee's emotional state, but you can observe changes in their professional engagement.

- Shift from "Proactive" to "Reactive": The employee still delivers high-quality work and meets all deadlines, but they no longer bring new ideas to the table, volunteer for projects, or engage in strategic discussions beyond their core duties.

- Drop in "Discretionary Effort": They stop doing the "extras" that once defined them—mentoring junior colleagues, sharing insightful articles, organizing team events.

- A "Competent but Quiet" Presence: In meetings, they are present and can answer direct questions flawlessly, but they are no longer an active part of the creative or collaborative energy of the team.

How to Intervene: The Manager's Script

A direct conversation is necessary, but it must be framed around performance and support, not diagnosis.

1. Acknowledge Their Contribution: Start by validating their work. "Anthony, I want to be clear that your performance remains excellent, and your work is valued."

2. State Your Neutral Observation: Link your observation to team dynamics or professional engagement. "I've noticed that in

our last few team meetings, we haven't heard as much from you during the brainstorming sessions. Your voice has always been a key part of how we innovate, and its absence is felt."

3. Offer Support and Resources (This is your primary goal): Open the door without demanding entry. "My job is to make sure you have the support you need not just to perform, but also to feel engaged and effective in your role. I want to make sure you're aware of the company's resources, like the Employee Assistance Program (EAP), which is a confidential support service. Is there anything I can do to help you reconnect with the parts of your work you've previously enjoyed?"

THE LEADER'S PRIMARY ROLE: RESOURCE, DON'T RESCUE

Your responsibility is to create a supportive environment and clearly point the way to professional resources (like HR or an EAP). You cannot "fix" the employee, and attempting to do so crosses a critical professional boundary. Your goal is to maintain a healthy team environment while providing the individual with the appropriate avenues for confidential support.

APPENDIX E:
THE SOCIETAL CRISIS OF NULLING OUT: A MANIFESTO FOR RECONNECTION

Nulling out is more than a personal tragedy. It is a cultural contagion. When our leaders, innovators, and professionals operate as highly efficient machines disconnected from their own humanity, the institutions they lead become hollowed-out as well. This appendix explores the architecture of this crisis and, more importantly, outlines the path to a collective reconnection.

THE ENGINE OF IMPLOSION: A DESPERATE SEARCH FOR FEELING

The destructive behaviors described in this book—the affair, the financial recklessness, the self-sabotage—are not random. They are the predictable consequences of a life optimized into a sterile void. They are a desperate, subconscious attempt to force a genuine emotional experience when all other routes have been closed. These implosions are not a failure of control; they are a tragic, last-ditch search for any authentic impulse worth controlling.

THE ORGANIZATIONAL IMPACT: A CONTAGION OF DISCONNECTION

Nulled-out leaders create nulled-out cultures. They reward emotional control and mistake passionate engagement for unprofessionalism. This "contagion effect" spreads, training new generations to optimize themselves in the same way. The result is an organization with a profound learning disability: it executes existing strategies brilliantly but loses the capacity for breakthrough innovation, which requires messy, authentic, human engagement. Ethical standards erode, not through malice, but through a systemic disconnection from the moral feelings that make ethics relevant.

THE TIPPING POINT: A CRISIS THAT HIDES IN PLAIN SIGHT

Nulling out follows the dangerous pattern of other systemic crises like the opioid epidemic or climate change: the damage happens gradually and invisibly until it reaches a catastrophic tipping point.

- Unlike addiction, it doesn't announce itself through dysfunction, but through an eerie, flawless functionality.

- Unlike the traditional mental health crisis, it doesn't generate obvious suffering, but an absence of it that is even more profound.

- The cumulative effect threatens our collective capacity for the wisdom-informed leadership that complex times demand.

WHY OUR SYSTEMS FAIL: TREATING THE SYMPTOM, NOT THE DISEASE

When a nulled-out individual finally implodes, our systems are designed to treat the aftermath, not the cause. The affair is treated as a problem of lust. The embezzlement is treated as a problem of greed. These interventions fail because they misdiagnose the core issue. The problem isn't a lack of control; it's a lack of a self worth controlling.

Our systems often reinforce the very optimization patterns that created the void in the first place, teaching the person to be even better at performing normalcy.

THE PATH FORWARD: A SYSTEMIC MANIFESTO FOR RECONNECTION

The most dangerous aspect of societal nulling out is that it eliminates the very capacities needed to solve the problem. But the window for intervention is now. The solution cannot be a series of individual fixes; it must be as systemic as the crisis itself. This is a blueprint for building a culture of reconnection at every level.

1. BUILDING COMMUNITIES OF SUPPORT: THE RECONNECTION ECOSYSTEM

The journey back from a nulled-out state is profoundly isolating. Therefore, the most powerful intervention is the creation of peer-led support networks that make authenticity feel normal and valuable, rather than a constant, lonely struggle.

- **Peer Support Coalitions ("Al-Anon for the Nulled-Out"):** Create con-fidential spaces for individuals to share experiences without judgment.

  o For Those in Recovery: A space for men and women who have been through it to support others just be-ginning. They offer the one thing no therapist can: the lived experience and credible hope that reconnection is possible.

  o For Spouses and Partners: A separate, dedicated space to share the unique challenges of loving a nulled-out person, breaking the isolation and gaslighting effect.

- **Professional Community Development:** Actively seek and create professional communities that value integration over pure op-timization.

  o Industry Groups: Focus on meaningful impact, not just efficiency metrics.

  o Professional Networks: Treat values-based decision-making as sophisticated, not naive.

  o Mentorship: Connect with leaders who have success-fully integrated authenticity with high performance.

- The Family Integration Project: Consciously design household dynamics that encourage genuine expression alongside responsible behavior. This means decision-making that honors both practical needs and individual preferences, creating a model of integrated living for the next generation.

2. A NEW LEADERSHIP PLAYBOOK: THE ORGANIZATIONAL DESIGN REVOLUTION

Leaders must be trained to recognize and reward wholeness, not just flawless execution. This means creating psychological safety for employees to express passion, dissent, and even vulnerability. It requires shifting our definition of a "star performer" from the one who is most controlled to the one who is most present: a fundamental redesign of the systems that define success.

- Hire for Integration: Recruit based on values alignment and authentic leadership capability, not just technical competence.

- Rethink Performance Management: Performance reviews must include questions about meaningful value creation, not just metric achievement. Promotion processes must evaluate inspirational authenticity, not just strategic optimization.

- Align Compensation with Sustainable Value: Reward the sustainable excellence that comes from authentic investment, not just the short-term results achieved through disconnected execution.

- Translate Authenticity into the Language of Business: Advocate for outcomes that honor authentic values by framing them in terms the organization understands: "sustainable performance," "long-term value creation," and "employee engagement metrics." This is not deception; it is translation.

3. THE LONG-TERM VISION: CREATING SYSTEMS THAT SUPPORT, NOT UNDERMINE

The ultimate goal is to create a culture where reconnection is unnecessary because disconnection never occurs in the first place.

- **The Educational Imperative:** Influence educational institutions to teach an integrated model of success. Business schools must teach strategic thinking that includes ethical reasoning. Pro-fessional programs must emphasize both technical compe-tence and values-based decision-making.

- **The Cultural Norm Shift:** As integrated success becomes more visible, cultural norms will shift. Media must feature success stories of both achievement and authentic engagement. In-dustry publications must celebrate innovations that serve mul-tiple stakeholders, not just efficient execution.

- **The Institutional Support Infrastructure:** Develop training pro-grams, leadership development, and research initiatives that document and teach the effectiveness of integrated ap-proaches, building a permanent foundation for a new kind of success.

The work begins by questioning what we have celebrated as professional excellence and seeing it for what it often is: a systematic self-erasure disguised as success. The path forward is not about "fixing" broken individuals, but about building a world where it is safe for them to show up whole.

APPENDIX F:
FURTHER READING AND RESEARCH

CORE TEXTS ON RELATED PHENOMENA ◆ BOOKS THAT UNDERSTAND HIGH-ACHIEVER DISCONNECTION

a. THE PARADOX OF CHOICE BY BARRY SCHWARTZ

- Explores how optimization can undermine satisfaction

- Relevant to understanding decision-making patterns in nulling out

- Provides research on why strategic analysis without authentic preference leads to emptiness

b. DRIVE BY DANIEL PINK

- Research on intrinsic vs. extrinsic motivation

- Essential for understanding why optimization-based success feels hollow

- Framework for reconnecting with authentic motivation

c. FLOW: THE PSYCHOLOGY OF OPTIMAL EXPERIENCE BY MIHALY CSIKSZENTMIHALYI

- Describes authentic engagement vs. performance-based activity

- Provides research foundation for understanding genuine satisfaction
- Practical approaches for finding activities that generate real engagement

d. ESSENTIALISM BY GREG MCKEOWN

- Strategic approach to choosing what matters vs. optimizing everything
- Useful for learning to make decisions based on values alongside efficiency
- Practical for high achievers who need frameworks for integration

RESEARCH ON MEANING AND WORK

a. MAN'S SEARCH FOR MEANING BY VIKTOR FRANKL

- Foundational text on purpose and meaning in human experience
- Relevant for understanding why success without meaning creates emptiness
- Philosophical framework for reconnection work

b. THE PURPOSE-DRIVEN LIFE BY RICK WARREN

- Practical approach to values clarification and purpose identification
- Useful for individuals beginning reconnection work
- Framework for integrating spiritual/philosophical purpose with daily life

c. AUTHENTIC HAPPINESS BY MARTIN SELIGMAN

- Research foundation for positive psychology and life satisfaction
- Distinguishes between hedonic and eudaimonic well-being
- Scientific backing for approaches that integrate achievement with meaning

ACADEMIC RESEARCH AND STUDIES PSYCHOLOGICAL RESEARCH RELEVANT TO NULLING OUT

a. BURNOUT VS. ENGAGEMENT RESEARCH:

- Maslach, C., & Leiter, M. P. (2016). Understanding the Burnout Experience
- Schaufeli, W. B., & Bakker, A. B. (2004). Job Demands, Job Resources, and Their Relationship with Burnout and Engagement
- Note: This research helps distinguish burnout from nulling out

b. INTRINSIC MOTIVATION RESEARCH:

- Deci, E. L., & Ryan, R. M. (2000). The "What" and "Why" of Goal Pursuits
- Ryan, R. M., & Deci, E. L. (2000). "Self-Determination Theory and the Facilitation of Intrinsic Motivation"
- Essential for understanding authentic vs. optimized motivation

c. VALUES AND LIFE SATISFACTION:

- Rokeach, M. (1973). The Nature of Human Values

- Schwartz, S. H. (1992). Universals in the Content and Structure of Values

- Research foundation for values-based decision-making

ORGANIZATIONAL PSYCHOLOGY RESEARCH

a. EMPLOYEE ENGAGEMENT STUDIES:

- Gallup's "State of the Global Workplace" (annual reports)

- Towers Watson "Global Workforce Study"

- Research showing high performance with low engagement (relevant to organizational nulling out)

b. LEADERSHIP AND AUTHENTICITY RESEARCH:

- George, B. (2003). Authentic Leadership: Rediscovering the Secrets to Creating Lasting Value

- Avolio, B. J., & Gardner, W. L. (2005). Authentic Leadership Development

- Research on leadership effectiveness through authentic vs. optimized approaches

PHILOSOPHICAL AND SPIRITUAL TEXTS

WORKS ON AUTHENTICITY AND INTEGRATION

a. BEING AND TIME BY MARTIN HEIDEGGER

- Philosophical foundation for understanding authentic vs. inauthentic existence
- Complex but foundational for understanding nulling out philosophically
- Best approached with secondary literature for practical application

b. THE GIFTS OF IMPERFECTION BY BRENÉ BROWN

- Practical approach to vulnerability and authenticity
- Useful for high achievers learning to integrate imperfection with excellence
- Research-based approach to authentic living

c. A NEW EARTH BY ECKHART TOLLE

- Spiritual perspective on ego-driven vs. authentic living
- Relevant for understanding identification with roles vs. authentic self
- Practical for individuals seeking spiritual frameworks for integration

EASTERN PHILOSOPHY AND INTEGRATION

d. THE TAO OF PHYSICS BY FRITJOF CAPRA

- Integration of analytical thinking with holistic understanding
- Useful for high achievers who need frameworks that honor both strategic thinking and broader wisdom

e. ZEN MIND, BEGINNER'S MIND BY SHUNRYU SUZUKI

- Approach to maintaining fresh perspective despite expertise
- Relevant for preventing optimization from deadening authentic response

BUSINESS AND LEADERSHIP LITERATURE

BOOKS ON INTEGRATED LEADERSHIP

a. GOOD TO GREAT BY JIM COLLINS

- Research on sustainable vs. optimization-focused leadership
- Relevant for understanding long-term effectiveness through integration
- Case studies of leaders who maintained authenticity alongside excellence

b. THE 7 HABITS OF HIGHLY EFFECTIVE PEOPLE BY STEPHEN COVEY

- Framework for principle-based vs. efficiency-based living
- Practical for individuals learning to integrate values with effectiveness
- Time-tested approach to sustainable success

c. START WITH WHY BY SIMON SINEK

- Framework for purpose-driven vs. optimization-driven approaches
- Practical for reconnecting with authentic motivation in professional contexts
- Useful for leaders creating integrated organizational cultures

ORGANIZATIONAL CULTURE AND CHANGE

a. TRIBAL LEADERSHIP BY DAVE LOGAN, JOHN KING, AND HALEE FISCHER-WRIGHT

- Framework for organizational cultures that support vs. undermine human engagement
- Relevant for creating environments that prevent nulling out
- Practical for leaders working to transform organizational culture

b. THE ADVANTAGE BY PATRICK LENCIONI

- Approach to organizational health that includes both performance and human factors

- Framework for creating integrated organizational cultures
- Practical for leaders balancing efficiency with employee engagement

SCIENTIFIC RESEARCH ON WELL-BEING AND PERFORMANCE

NEUROSCIENCE AND PSYCHOLOGY

a. THE HAPPINESS HYPOTHESIS BY JONATHAN HAIDT

- Research synthesis on factors that create genuine vs. superficial satisfaction
- Scientific foundation for understanding why optimization without meaning fails
- Practical applications for reconnection work

b. MINDSET BY CAROL DWECK

- Research on growth vs. fixed mindsets
- Relevant for approaching reconnection work with appropriate expectations
- Framework for learning integration skills

c. THE PARADOX OF DECLINING FEMALE HAPPINESS BY BETSEY STEVENSON AND JUSTIN WOLFERS

- Research showing that improved external conditions don't automatically create satisfaction
- Relevant for understanding why optimized life circumstances can feel empty

- Economic research applicable to nulling out phenomenon

LONGITUDINAL STUDIES

a. HARVARD STUDY OF ADULT DEVELOPMENT:

- Long-term research on factors that create life satisfaction
- Findings relevant to relationship quality vs. achievement focus
- Available through Harvard's website and various publications

b. GRANT STUDY RESULTS:

- George Vaillant's Triumphs of Experience
- Long-term research on what creates sustainable satisfaction vs. temporary achievement
- Relevant for understanding integration vs. optimization approaches

PRACTICAL ASSESSMENT AND DEVELOPMENT TOOLS

VALUES ASSESSMENT RESOURCES

a. VIA CHARACTER STRENGTHS SURVEY:

- Scientific assessment of character strengths
- Useful for identifying authentic strengths vs. optimized capabilities
- Available online with extensive research backing

b. ROKEACH VALUE SURVEY:

- Classic values assessment tool

- Helpful for clarifying authentic values vs. adopted expectations

- Available through various psychology and coaching resources

PROFESSIONAL DEVELOPMENT ASSESSMENTS

a. STRENGTHS FINDER 2.0:

- Assessment of natural talents vs. developed skills

- Useful for distinguishing authentic capabilities from optimization

- Practical for career development that honors natural strengths

b. MYERS-BRIGGS TYPE INDICATOR (MBTI):

- Assessment of natural preferences vs. adapted behaviors

- Relevant for understanding authentic personality vs. professional persona

- Best used with qualified practitioner interpretation

ONLINE RESOURCES AND CONTINUING EDUCATION

RESEARCH DATABASES

a. PSYCINFO AND PSYCHOLOGY DATABASES:

- Academic research on related topics

- Available through university libraries and some public libraries

- Search terms: "work engagement," "authentic leadership," "intrinsic motivation," "values and satisfaction"

b. GOOGLE SCHOLAR:

- Free access to academic research

- Search for recent studies on employee engagement, leadership authenticity, values-based decision-making

PROFESSIONAL DEVELOPMENT PLATFORMS

a. TED TALKS AND TEDX:

- Talks on purpose, meaning, authentic leadership

- Search for speakers discussing integration of success with satisfaction

- Many talks available free online

b. LINKEDIN LEARNING AND SIMILAR PLATFORMS:

- Courses on authentic leadership, values-based decision-making

- Professional development that includes meaning alongside efficiency

- Filter for courses that address integration rather than just optimization

JOURNALS AND ONGOING RESEARCH

ACADEMIC JOURNALS

a. JOURNAL OF BUSINESS ETHICS

- Research on values-based business decisions
- Relevant for integrating ethics with strategic thinking

b. APPLIED PSYCHOLOGY: HEALTH AND WELL-BEING

- Research on workplace satisfaction and engagement
- Studies relevant to preventing and addressing professional emptiness

c. LEADERSHIP QUARTERLY

- Research on authentic vs. transactional leadership
- Studies on sustainable leadership approaches

INDUSTRY PUBLICATIONS

a. HARVARD BUSINESS REVIEW

- Regular articles on meaning, purpose, and authentic leadership
- Case studies of integrated approaches to business challenges
- Search their archives for "purpose," "authentic leadership," "employee engagement"

b. MIT SLOAN MANAGEMENT REVIEW

- Research-based articles on organizational culture and leadership
- Often includes studies relevant to integration vs. optimization

WARNINGS ABOUT POTENTIALLY UNHELPFUL RESOURCES

AVOID RESOURCES THAT:

- Treat nulling out as standard depression or anxiety
- Promote dramatic life changes without integration work
- Focus only on work-life balance without addressing authenticity
- Oversimplify complex integration challenges
- Promise quick fixes to deep disconnection patterns
- Dismiss the importance of continued professional competence

USE CAUTION WITH:

- Self-help books that don't understand high-achiever dynamics
- Spiritual texts that dismiss practical responsibilities
- Business books that focus only on optimization
- Therapy approaches that pathologize optimization skills
- Online forums without professional moderation

Remember: The goal is finding resources that support integration of authenticity with continued excellence, not choosing between success and satisfaction.

APPENDIX G:
EMERGENCY RESOURCES FOR CRISIS SITUATIONS

IMMEDIATE CRISIS SUPPORT IF YOU'RE HAVING THOUGHTS OF SELF-HARM OR SUICIDE

UNITED STATES:

- **National Suicide Prevention Lifeline: 988**
  - o 24/7 confidential support
  - o Available in English and Spanish
  - o Chat option available at suicidepreventionlifeline.org
- **Crisis Text Line: Text HOME to 741741**
  - o 24/7 text-based crisis support
  - o Trained crisis counselors
  - o Free and confidential

INTERNATIONAL:

- **International Association for Suicide Prevention: https://iasp.info**
- **Befrienders Worldwide: befrienders.org**
- **Crisis lines by country: findahelpline.com**

IF YOU'RE EXPERIENCING IMMEDIATE MENTAL HEALTH CRISIS

WHEN TO GO TO AN EMERGENCY ROOM:

- Thoughts of harming yourself or others
- Complete inability to function in daily life
- Severe panic or anxiety that won't subside
- Feeling completely disconnected from reality
- Any situation where you feel unsafe

WHAT TO TELL EMERGENCY MEDICAL STAFF:

- "I'm experiencing a mental health crisis"
- Describe specific symptoms (not functioning, thoughts of harm, etc.)
- Mention if you're taking any medications
- Ask for a mental health evaluation

PROFESSIONAL EMERGENCY RESOURCES

24/7 PROFESSIONAL CRISIS LINES

a. SAMHSA NATIONAL HELPLINE: 1-800-662-4357

- Substance Abuse and Mental Health Services Administration
- 24/7 treatment referral service
- Information for individuals facing mental health crises
- Available in English and Spanish

b. NATIONAL ALLIANCE ON MENTAL ILLNESS (NAMI) HELPLINE: 1-800-950-6264

- Monday–Friday, 10 a.m.–10 p.m. ET

- Information, referrals, and support

- Email: info@nami.org

PROFESSIONAL EMERGENCY SERVICES

a. MOBILE CRISIS TEAMS:

- Many areas have mobile mental health crisis response

- Call 911 and request mental health crisis team if available

- Alternative to emergency room for non-life-threatening crises

b. PSYCHIATRIC EMERGENCY SERVICES:

- Many hospitals have specialized psychiatric emergency departments

- Call ahead to verify availability

- May have shorter wait times than general emergency room

CRISIS SITUATIONS SPECIFIC TO NULLING OUT

i. WHEN DESPERATE ATTEMPTS TO FEEL SOMETHING BECOME DANGEROUS

WARNING SIGNS OF CRISIS-LEVEL NULLING OUT:

- Engaging in increasingly reckless behavior to feel anything
- Complete inability to access any authentic responses
- Making decisions that could destroy career, relationships, or finances just to feel consequences
- Feeling like you've completely disappeared from your own life
- Persistent thoughts that nothing matters or has meaning

IMMEDIATE STEPS:

1. Remove yourself from situations where you might make destructive decisions.
2. Contact someone who knows you well and can provide perspective.
3. Avoid major decisions until you can access professional support.
4. Use crisis resources if you're feeling unsafe or completely out of control.

ii. PROFESSIONAL SELF-SABOTAGE CRISIS

IF YOU'RE ABOUT TO OR HAVE:

- Destroyed important professional relationships
- Made financial decisions that threaten your security

- Engaged in behavior that could end your career

- Violated professional ethics or legal boundaries

IMMEDIATE ACTIONS:

1. Stop the behavior immediately.

2. Contact a lawyer if legal issues are involved.

3. Reach out to a trusted mentor or colleague for perspective.

4. Seek immediate professional support to understand what's happening.

5. Don't make additional major decisions until you have support.

iii. RELATIONSHIP AND FAMILY CRISIS RESOURCES

IF YOUR NULLING OUT IS DESTROYING YOUR FAMILY

a. NATIONAL DOMESTIC VIOLENCE HOTLINE: 1-800-799-7233

- If disconnection has led to any form of domestic violence

- 24/7 confidential support

- Available in multiple languages

b. FAMILY CRISIS COUNSELING:

- Search for "family crisis counseling" in your area.

- Many areas have emergency family counseling services.

- Employee Assistance Programs often provide immediate family support.

iv. WHEN CHILDREN ARE AFFECTED

IF YOUR NULLING OUT IS IMPACTING YOUR CHILDREN:

- Contact school counselors who can provide immediate support for children.
- Reach out to family members who can provide temporary additional support.
- Seek immediate family therapy to address crisis before long-term damage occurs.
- Consider temporary arrangements that ensure children's emotional safety while you get help.

v. FINANCIAL CRISIS RESOURCES

IF DESTRUCTIVE BEHAVIOR HAS CREATED FINANCIAL EMERGENCY

a. NATIONAL FOUNDATION FOR CREDIT COUNSELING: 1-800-388-2227

- Nonprofit credit counseling services
- Help with debt management and financial crisis
- Available if reckless financial behavior has created crisis

b. EMPLOYEE ASSISTANCE PROGRAMS (EAP):

- Many employers provide financial counseling through EAP
- Often includes crisis financial planning
- Usually confidential and free

vi. IF YOU'VE ENGAGED IN FINANCIAL MISCONDUCT

IMMEDIATE STEPS:

1. Stop all questionable financial behavior immediately.

2. Contact a lawyer specializing in financial/corporate law.

3. Do not destroy any documents.

4. Seek immediate psychological support to understand the behavior.

5. Consider voluntary disclosure if illegal activity is involved.

vii. WORKPLACE CRISIS RESOURCES

IF NULLING OUT IS CAUSING PROFESSIONAL CRISIS

a. HUMAN RESOURCES DEPARTMENT:

- If your behavior is affecting work performance

- Many companies have mental health resources

- May provide leave options while you seek help

b. EMPLOYEE ASSISTANCE PROGRAMS (EAP):

- Confidential counseling services

- Often include crisis intervention

- Usually available 24/7

- Free through most employers

viii. PROFESSIONAL ETHICS VIOLATIONS

IF YOU'VE VIOLATED PROFESSIONAL ETHICS:

1. Stop the behavior immediately.
2. Contact your professional licensing board for guidance.
3. Seek legal counsel if necessary.
4. Get immediate psychological support.
5. Consider voluntary reporting if required by your profession.

ix. SUPPORT FOR FAMILY MEMBERS AND COLLEAGUES

IF SOMEONE YOU KNOW IS NULLED-OUT AND IN CRISIS

WARNING SIGNS TO WATCH FOR:

- Sudden dramatic changes in behavior or decision-making
- Engaging in uncharacteristic risky behavior
- Expressing feelings of complete emptiness or meaninglessness
- Making decisions that seem designed to destroy what they've built
- Talking about feeling like they've disappeared from their own life

HOW TO HELP:

1. Express concern without judgment.
2. Don't try to fix or analyze the situation.
3. Encourage professional help.

4. Offer practical support (childcare, transportation to appointments).

5. Contact crisis resources if they express thoughts of self-harm.

x. WHEN TO INVOLVE OTHERS

CONTACT CRISIS SERVICES IF SOMEONE IS:

- Expressing thoughts of suicide or self-harm

- Engaging in behavior that puts them or others in immediate danger

- Completely unable to care for themselves or their dependents

- Making threats toward others

- Showing signs of complete psychological breakdown

CREATING YOUR PERSONAL CRISIS PLAN

BEFORE CRISIS OCCURS

1. IDENTIFY YOUR SUPPORT NETWORK:

- List 3–5 people you can contact in crisis.

- Include their phone numbers.

- Make sure they understand they're part of your crisis plan.

2. CHOOSE YOUR PROFESSIONAL RESOURCES:

- Identify therapist or coach who understands nulling out.

- Have contact information readily available.

- Know location of nearest psychiatric emergency services.

3. PLAN FOR COMMON CRISIS SCENARIOS:

- What you'll do if you feel like making destructive professional decisions

- Who you'll call if you're feeling completely empty and desperate

- How you'll handle urges to engage in reckless behavior

CRISIS PLAN TEMPLATE

WHEN I NOTICE WARNING SIGNS OF CRISIS (FILL IN YOUR SPECIFIC SIGNS):I WILL IMMEDIATELY:

1. Contact: _____ (phone: _____)

2. Go to: _____ (location: _____)

3. Avoid: _____ (specific triggers or situations)

My professional crisis contact:

_____

_____

My personal crisis contact:

_____

_____

My medical crisis contact:

_____

_____

EMERGENCY NUMBERS TO CALL:

- Crisis line:

_____

_____

- Therapist/coach:

_____

_____

- Trusted friend/family:

_____

_____

RECOVERY AFTER CRISIS

a. AFTER IMMEDIATE CRISIS IS RESOLVED

IMMEDIATE STEPS:

1. Continue professional support—crisis resolution isn't recovery.

2. Assess damage from crisis behaviors calmly with professional help.

3. Create plan for addressing consequences of crisis actions.

4. Begin systematic reconnection work to address underlying nulling out.

5. Strengthen crisis prevention plan based on what triggered the crisis.

b. LONG-TERM RECOVERY:

- Crisis often provides motivation for serious reconnection work.

- Use crisis experience as information about what happens when nulling out isn't addressed.

- Focus on integration work to prevent future crises.

- Consider sharing your experience to help others recognize warning signs.

IMPORTANT REMINDERS

CRISIS IS NOT FAILURE:

- Crisis often occurs when nulling out reaches unbearable levels.

- It can be the wake-up call needed to begin serious reconnection work.

- Many people who recover from nulling out experienced crisis first.

PROFESSIONAL HELP IS ESSENTIAL:

- Crisis-level nulling out usually requires professional support

- Self-help approaches aren't sufficient during crisis

- Recovery is possible with appropriate professional guidance

CRISIS PASSES:

- The intensity of crisis is temporary.

- Professional help can provide immediate stabilization.

- Long-term recovery is possible with appropriate support.

YOU'RE NOT ALONE:

- Many high-achievers experience crisis-level nulling out.

- Professional resources understand this phenomenon.

- Recovery and integration are achievable with.

Remember: If you're in immediate danger, call 911 or go to your nearest emergency room. These resources are here to help you through crisis toward recovery and integration.

ACKNOWLEDGEMENTS:

A book is never a solo journey. Crafting this second edition of Nulling Out has been a labor of love and wouldn't be possible without the talented team who has assisted me in bringing you the book you now hold.

My deepest thanks to my editorial team who challenged, polished, and championed this manuscript at every stage: Melissa Woods, Ezra Linehan, and Elizabeth Caleca. Your insights were invaluable.

To my brilliant cover and interior designers: Aaniyah Ahmed, Kostis Pavlou, and Krishna Mohan. Thank you for creating a visual soul for this book and workbook.

To Ian Bright: thank you for transforming my images for chapter 3 into beautiful, clear graphics that are the heart of Chapter 3.

To the late Dr. Frank Menolascino, my mentor and personal champion: it was you who recognized this as my field, and you were absolutely right. I will always hold you in the highest regard. And, I miss you.

And last but certainly not least, I thank you, God, for guiding me to this concept—something that was right in front of me, a thought I longed to put into words. You brought all of the creative minds mentioned above into my life to help me craft this work and bless the world. Thank you, Sir

ABOUT THE AUTHOR

No one is immune to the human condition. Least of all a doctor who spends her life inside it.

My journey as a physician has spanned four decades, from the shores of Maine to the beaches of Hawaii, through settings as diverse as primary care, forensics, and correctional medicine. But my most profound education and unique vantage point didn't come from a textbook. It came from the trenches and from my own life. It provided me a front-row seat to what conventional frameworks were failing to address.

My personal journey provided my compass. My professional journey—working with thousands of lives, from the salt-of-the-earth to the titans of industry—provided the map. It was from this unique vantage point that I identified the silent epidemic of high-functioning emptiness and gave it a name: "nulling out." But for me, this was never just a clinical observation.

The truth is, I know what it's like to build a life that looks perfect on the outside, only to look in the mirror and not recognize the person staring back. I have been nulled-out before. I have also recovered from burnout—twice. I'm not just a doctor who has studied these conditions; I'm a human being who has navigated the darkness and found the path back to the light.

This erasure of the self is not a psychiatric illness to be medicated, but a profound spiritual crisis born from a life of optimization over authenticity. From this synthesis of lived experience and clinical observation, I pioneered the integrative approach this book details: a path for successful men to reclaim their internal fire without destroying everything they've built.

This book is the culmination of that entire journey. It is the synthesis of rigorous professional knowledge and hard-won personal wisdom.

My mission is to help men feel as alive on the inside as they appear accomplished on the outside.